HMS *BRISTOL*

HMS BRISTOL

In a Class of Her Own

Rob Griffin

Published in Great Britain by Gallantry Books

an imprint of Mortons Books Ltd.

Media Centre

Morton Way

Horncastle LN9 6JR

www.mortonsbooks.co.uk

ISBN978-1-911658-75-7

The right of Robert Griffin to be identified as the author of this work has been asserted in accordance with the Copyright, Designs and Patents Act 1988.

Design by: Druck Media Pvt. Ltd.

CONTENTS

Judi Mair Bowes 1973–2022

THE BEGINNING

Lady Hogg has broken the champagne and sent HMS *Bristol* down the slipway at Swan Hunter's yard. (Tyne & Wear Archives & Museums)

HMS *Bristol*'s beginnings are very closely tied in to the state of the Royal Navy's Fleet Air Arm requirements at the beginning of the 1960s; at this time the Royal Navy still had one of the largest carrier fleets in the world, and was second only to the US Navy who, having realised the value of the aircraft carrier, was gearing up to start building 80,000-ton Kitty Hawk-class aircraft carriers, which were designed to carry up to 90 aircraft, a figure which made the Royal Navy carriers look very outmoded.

The British fleet at that time included the fleet carriers *Ark Royal* and *Eagle*, with two smaller carriers, the completely reconstructed *Victorious* and the much newer light carrier *Hermes*, both with 3D Type 984 radar but limited to air groups of 25 aircraft – at the most 20 fighters and strike aircraft and five helicopters or alternatively 16 fighters and strike aircraft and four AEW Gannet turboprops and five helicopters. A fifth carrier, *Centaur*, was modernised to the minimum standard to operate second-

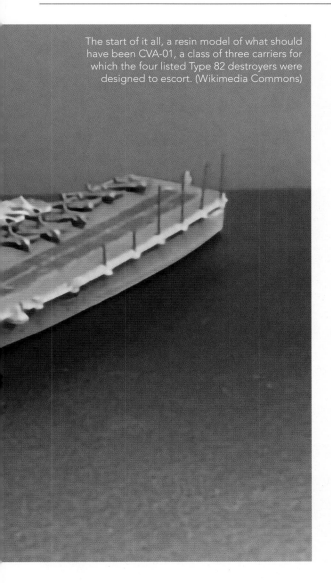

The start of it all, a resin model of what should have been CVA-01, a class of three carriers for which the four listed Type 82 destroyers were designed to escort. (Wikimedia Commons)

as its new fleet air defence aircraft. With the remainder of the air group this would give a total of approximately 40 aircraft, which compared poorly to the 95 available to a Kitty Hawk-class ship. The increasing weight and size of modern jet fighters meant that a larger deck area was required for take-offs and landings. Although the Royal Navy had come up with increasingly innovative ways to allow ever larger aircraft to operate from the small flight decks of their carriers, the limited physical life left in the existing ships – with only *Hermes* being considered capable of reliable and efficient extension past 1975, and the inability of both *Victorious* and *Hermes*, the most effectively and expensively modernised of the carriers to operate the F-4 or a useful number of Buccaneers – motivated the need to order and build at least two (although four was the number that the navy would have hoped to build) new large fleet carriers.

As always there were the usual battles with the Treasury and the War Office, and in the background the RAF fighting to convince everyone that land based could do anything that a carrier could but for a lot less. However, once the Chiefs of Staff had given their approval to the idea of new carriers being necessary, in January 1962, in the strategic paper COS (621)1, 'British Strategy in the Sixties', the Admiralty Board had to sift through six possible designs. These ranged from 42,000 to 68,000 tons at full load. One design was based on the American Forrestal class, but was rejected early on as being significantly too costly, particularly in terms of the dockyard upgrades that would be needed to service them.

The advantages of size were immediately apparent; a 42,000-ton carrier could only hold 27 aircraft, while a 55,000-ton carrier could carry forty-nine. This was an 80 per cent increase in the size of the air group for a 30 per cent increase in displacement. Even with these smaller designs cost was a serious issue. The Treasury and the Air Ministry were pushing for a new set of long-range strike aircraft operating from a string of bases around the globe.

generation Scimitars and Vixens in 1959 but was never satisfactory or safe for operating nuclear strike aircraft and was a purely interim capability while *Eagle* was refitting.

While *Ark Royal*, *Eagle*, *Hermes* and *Bulwark* were all capable of operating the S.2 version of the Blackburn Buccaneer strike aircraft, only *Ark Royal* and *Eagle* were realistically big enough to accommodate both a squadron of Buccaneers (up to 14 aircraft) and a squadron of F-4 Phantoms, which the Royal Navy intended to procure

This is from the ship's books and is one of a series of images taken on board by the now defunct Swan Hunter's. These provide an interesting look at the ship as built and in pristine condition. (HMS *Bristol*)

Success and HMS *Bristol* gets wet for the first time; this also give a good idea of what the slipway looks like. (Tyne & Wear Archives & Museums)

A view not often seen of any warship, this is *Bristol* in dry dock, showing two of her three stabilisers and the bilge keel; it would seem that the alignment of the stabilisers is being checked out. (HMS *Bristol*)

Port rear view looking forward showing the 4.5-inch gun turret; note the anti-slip panels on the deck. (HMS *Bristol*)

The resulting carriers were to be named the Queen Elizabeth class, and originally there were to be four in the class, although this very soon was reduced to three. Interestingly the lead vessel, CVA-01, was officially named *Queen Elizabeth* before any steel was cut, this honour being granted by Her Majesty. The other two names are more speculation than confirmed but the favourites seemed to be *Duke of Edinburgh* and *Prince of Wales*.

The CVA-01 would have displaced 54,500 tons (although the ship was said to displace 53,000 tons 'in average action condition'), with a flight deck length (including the bridle arrester boom) of 963 feet 3 inches (293.6 metres). The size of the flight deck, combined with steam catapults and arrester gear, would have enabled the carriers to operate the latest jets.

The aircraft complement would have included 36 Phantom fighter/ground-attack aircraft and/or Buccaneer low-level strike aircraft, four early-warning aircraft, five anti-submarine helicopters and two search-and-rescue helicopters.

The large 'Broomstick' radar dome above the central island on the carrier was planned to be Type 988 Anglo-Dutch 3D radar, which would subsequently be fitted on the Royal Netherlands Navy Tromp-class frigates, although this would not have been fitted to the final carrier as Britain pulled out of the project. This was also projected for HMS *Bristol* as well and the drawings showing this make her look a really top-heavy ship.

So far so good. The navy looked as if it was going to get its new carriers and the Fleet Air Arm was safe. Parallel thinking also showed that the current fleet of destroyers and escorts

Looking astern, this shows the davits and associated boats before their removal later on. (HMS *Bristol*)

This shot on 1 deck shows the 36-foot work boat in its davits; years later these would be removed to allow a gun deck to be added with extra weapons as a result of the Falklands War experience. (HMS *Bristol*)

It seems a shame that very shortly this commissioning cake will be cut, traditionally by the sponsor (in this case Lady Hogg) and the youngest member of the crew. These cakes really are works of art. Also, silver that was presented to a previous HMS *Bristol* in 1911 can be seen; the decanters were presented by Lady Hogg and the candelabra by the city of Bristol. (HMS Bristol Association)

were not going to be suitable escorts for the new carriers – with most of them being either Second World War build or designed from that period, they would not be able to carry the new equipment and weapons expected to arrive in the fleet in the next decade or so. Various designs were examined and eventually what was to be known as the Type 82 class was decided on. This was to be a class of four (although some sources say six)

large destroyers, carrying the latest weapons fit and technology. The first, which became HMS *Bristol*, was ordered on 4 October 1966 and laid down on 15 November 1967 at Swan Hunter's yard and finally launched on 30 June 1969 at an estimated cost of £2,441,700.

For a while all looked good but in October 1964 a Labour government came to power; one of their first stated intentions was to cut back on defence and the carrier strike force

HMS *Bristol's* first captain, R. D. McDonald, reads out the commissioning warrant, traditionally done in front of the whole crew; it is a standard document, but the ceremony goes back centuries. This was a first for the Royal Navy, as it was the first time a ship had visited the place she was named after for commissioning. (HMS Bristol Association)

HMS *Bristol* soon after acceptance paid a visit to Avonmouth docks to accept an invitation from the Mayor of Bristol. (HMS Bristol Association)

was an easy target. Dennis Healey, the new Secretary of State for Defence, after hearing all the arguments for and against from all sides of the armed forces, eventually sided with the RAF, who again claimed that they could cover all operations by using land-based aircraft, at a fraction of the cost of carriers. This claim was proved false on several subsequent occasions and came to a head in the South Atlantic in 1982. One apocryphal tale relates that the RAF actually had maps produced that showed Australia moved by 500 miles to support the land-based theory. The RAF

also wanted funds to support their TSR2 programme and the follow-up purchase of the American F111 swing-wing bomber. It is said that the Navy case was argued very badly but I think no matter who had fought for the navy, it would have been a lost cause.

The blow came in the Defence White Paper 1966 which cancelled all the proposed new carriers as well as the remainder of the Type 82 escorts. HMS *Bristol*, however, was partially built and again arguments ranged back and forth: should she be scrapped or completed, and if completed what would

Who said that glamour is not allowed on a warship? This group of Sea Rangers certainly seem to be enjoying their visit to Bristol, during her stay at Avonmouth. (HMS Bristol Association)

Lady Hogg on a visit to the ship presents Captain McDonald CBE, ADC with a colour print of the Clifton area of Bristol. Lady Hogg was the ship's sponsor and launched her; one can but hope that these prints have been saved. (HMS Bristol Association)

The Ceremony

and

Order of Service

used in asking

The Blessing of Almighty God

upon the Commissioning of

Her Majesty's Ship Bristol

at Bristol   Saturday, 31st March, 1973

The front page of the order of service for the commissioning service of HMS *Bristol*, Saturday, 31 March 1973. (HMS Bristol Association)

The Lord Mayor of Bristol

requests the pleasure of the company of

at a Reception on Friday, 30th March, 1973
at The Council House, College Green,

on the occasion of the

Commissioning of Her Majesty's Ship "Bristol"

Please reply to :
Lord Mayor's Secretary,
The Council House,
College Green, Bristol, BS1 5TR

Uniform or
Lounge Suit
7.15—8.45 p.m.

The invitation from the Lord Mayor of Bristol inviting the ship's company to a reception on the occasion of her commissioning. (HMS Bristol Association)

her role be now that the carriers were not to be built? The government was also looking at building a smaller and less costly class of destroyers, and these would morph into the Type 42 destroyers of which 14 were eventually built. As for HMS *Bristol*, the decision was taken to complete her and trial the weapons and equipment she was due to have received originally – most of which would be fitted into the Type 42 and other ships anyway. It was thought this would probably give her a lifespan of around 10 years; she could then quietly be disposed of and the last remnants of the ambitious strike carrier force escorts could be buried. Who would have predicted that in 2019 she would still be in commissioned service albeit in a static role, having gone through a myriad of roles and earning herself the sobriquet 'One of a Kind and in a Class of her own'?

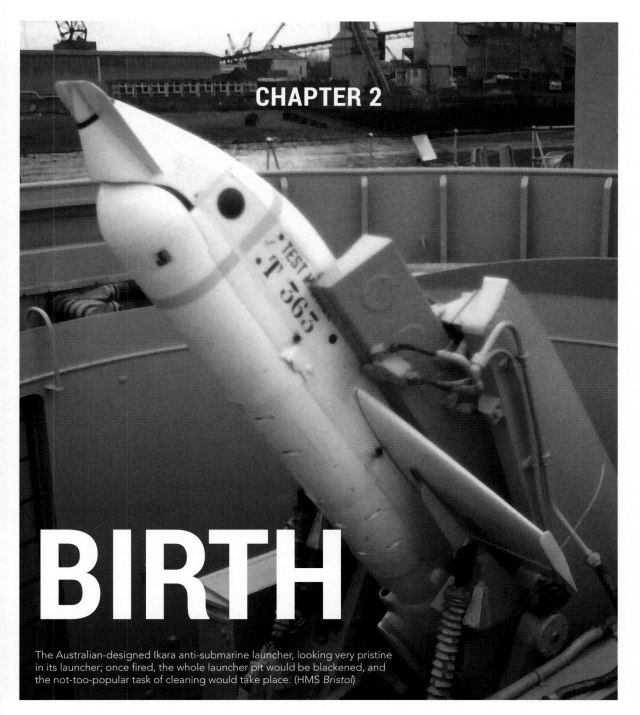

BIRTH

The Australian-designed Ikara anti-submarine launcher, looking very pristine in its launcher; once fired, the whole launcher pit would be blackened, and the not-too-popular task of cleaning would take place. (HMS *Bristol*)

As we have seen in the previous chapter, the fact that HMS *Bristol* actually made it to her launch date was very much a hit and miss affair; however, once the decision was taken to complete her for use as a trial ship, work carried on and she was ready for her launch on 30 June 1969; although it had been scheduled for 2 June, due to shipyard industrial action, the launch was delayed. She was however named on 2 June at a naming ceremony by Lady Hogg, accompanied by the city of Bristol's Lord Mayor and Lady Mayoress, Alderman Wilcox and his wife and the Sheriff and his wife. A similar sort of way of doing things was performed for the two new carriers. The drawing shows how she nearly ended up.

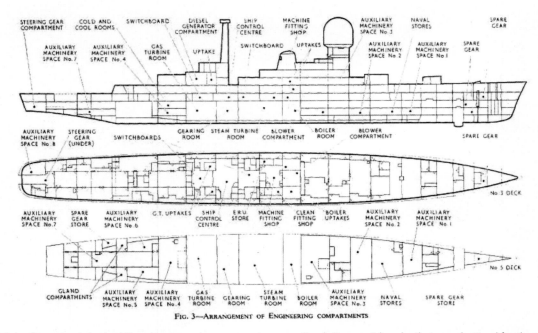

FIG. 3—ARRANGEMENT OF ENGINEERING COMPARTMENTS

What *Bristol* very nearly looked like; she was going to carry the same Dutch Broomstick radar that was destined for the CVA-01 carrier class. (HMS *Bristol*)

After her eventual launch *Bristol* was taken to the fitting-out berth where she would remain until the early part of 1973. This period was when all her fittings, equipment and armament were installed; even today with the modular approach to ship building, a lot of time is still spent in fitting out. During this period, the ship's officers and company started to arrive and were housed in the first instance at shore establishments before moving to more permanent accommodation on board. For department heads this was a frantic time liaising with the dockyard in order to get items in their department put into what were sensible locations to make life just that bit more manageable. In the end it all came down to a happy (mostly) compromise.

Finally, she was ready, and to honour the city from which she took her name, it was arranged by the Royal Navy that the formal commissioning ceremony would be held at Avonmouth just outside Bristol. This took place on 31 March 1973 and among the dignitaries were the Deputy Lord Mayor,

Bristol's first commanding officer, Captain Roderick MacDonald CBE, RN and the commissioning officer Vice-Admiral Sir Terrence Lewin RN (later Admiral of the Fleet Lord Lewin).

At last *Bristol* was afloat and fully manned and now officially part of the Royal Navy, but with the demise of the projected new carriers, what would become of her? The intention was to use her as a trial vessel for all the new equipment coming online. So, what had the Royal Navy actually got for its money? On first viewing the ship, the impression was that she was huge and nothing like the man in the street would imagine a destroyer to look like, most imagining destroyers to be small, fast vessels and, to some extent, regarding size, they are correct. For example, *Bristol* was 507 feet long (155 metres) compared to a Second World War destroyer such as HMS *Cossack* which was 377 feet (115 metres) in length; in fact, she was just smaller than a Second World War cruiser such as HMS *Exeter* of River Plate fame.

This is the base of one of two Corvus launcher systems that were fitted; these had seven launcher tubes that when fired dispersed chaff – foil strips cut to a set length to confuse the seeker systems on an incoming missile. (Rob Griffin)

Displacement: 6,400 tonnes (standard), 7,100 tonnes (full)
Length: 155 m (507 ft)
Beam: 17 m (55 ft)
Draught: 7.5 m (24 ft 7 in)
Propulsion: COSAG,* 2 standard-range geared steam turbines 30,000 hp (22,000 kW); 2 Bristol-Siddeley Olympus TM1A Gas turbines 30,000 hp, 2 shafts, 2 boilers
Speed : 28 knots (52 km/h)
Range: 5,750 nautical miles (10,650 km) at 18 knots (33 km/h)
Complement: 397 (incl. 30 officers)
Armament: Sea Dart ,Ikara 4.5-inch Mark 8 gun and Limbo mortar
Aircraft carried: none.
Aviation facilities: flight deck
Armament: Sea Dart ,Ikara 4.5-inch Mark 8 gun and Limbo mortar
Aircraft carried: none.
Aviation facilities: flight deck

* combined steam and gas

Although a flight deck is mentioned it was not strictly that and was only temporary, although helicopters could land. However, during the Falklands War the deck was strengthened to take the heavier helicopters in use then. The main reason that no hangar was included in any of the designs is, it was felt, that it was not needed as she would be operating with the large new fleet carriers. As launched, she was a very powerful fighting ship, even though the systems were new and untested at sea, which is vastly different from working during trials and development.

The use of COSAG would very soon prove to be a very sound decision and one that probably saved the ship from being scrapped when she was less than two years old: while she was anchored off Milford Haven, a fire broke out in the steam turbine room and boiler rooms. It took six hours of hard firefighting to finally bring the fire under control; even though she was eventually repaired, anyone visiting the ship today

can see if they carefully look, evidence of the temperatures generated. The bulkhead outside what is now the First Lieutenant's/XO's office has a discernible distortion to it caused by the fire. A recollection of that night comes from Bob Page:

> Forty-six years ago tonight, the starboard watch was just getting turned in after a run ashore in Milford Haven when all hell let loose. Alarms ringing. People shouting and over the Tannoy,

'Fire, fire, fire, fire in the engine room. Damage control and fire parties close up.' So began that eventful night which we all have different memories of. As one of the firefighting team who tried unsuccessfully to enter the engine room, I will always remember Halloween differently to all my civvy friends. Thanks to the Welsh fire brigade: without them I doubt Bristol would have survived to play the many roles she has had up to her decommissioning. Stay safe all my shipmates and oppos from that night.

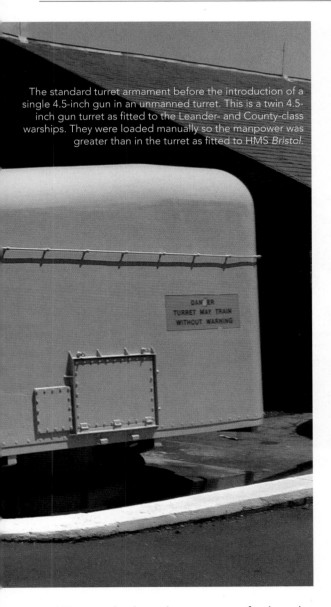

The standard turret armament before the introduction of a single 4.5-inch gun in an unmanned turret. This is a twin 4.5-inch gun turret as fitted to the Leander- and County-class warships. They were loaded manually so the manpower was greater than in the turret as fitted to HMS *Bristol*.

We now look at the weapons fit that she carried as built; like most warships this fit changed either as new weapons were introduced or ones become obsolete, or as a result of a conflict, such as the Falklands, which saw all Royal Navy ships lose all their traditional sea boats and have them replaced by additional weapons.

The first new weapon that was fitted to HMS *Bristol* was the new type 4.5-inch gun with a longer 55-calibre barrel; it was designed in the 1960s for the Royal Navy's new classes of frigates and destroyers. The 4.5-inch gun has been the standard medium-gun calibre of the Royal Navy for use against surface, aircraft, and shore targets since 1938. The 55-calibre Mark 8 gun replaced the Second World War-era 45-calibre QF 4.5-inch Mk I–V naval guns. It has a calibre of 4.45 inches (113 mm). The use of a single gun was a complete departure from tradition, for up till then ships would normally have had two or more turret-mounted in the super firing style and each turret would have had twin guns (although not always). The new weapon was built by Vickers Ltd Armament Division and was developed by the Royal Armament Research and Development Establishment using the Ordnance QF 105 mm L13 of the Abbot self-propelled gun as a starting point. The outer shell of the gun house was built from glass-reinforced plastic (GRP). It was another total departure from the norm gone were the armoured turrets with two guns, and in fact as this weapon has no crew inside, the cover really was protection against the elements.

The new weapon emphasised reliability and rapid response to fire first round from shutdown state, particularly for defence against missiles, over a high rate of fire, allowing a switch to a lighter, single barrel mounting and ammunition of a one-piece design.

The gun system had a combination of electrical and hydraulic components, and the full system penetrated up to three deck levels below the weather deck: deep magazine, gun control room and power room, gun bay and the turret.

The weapon was semi-automatic and could be operated by a smaller crew than its predecessors. With no personnel in the gun turret, loading was supported by personnel in the gun bay to load the feed ring and in the deep magazine to pass ammunition to the gun bay. The captain of the gun in the control room ensured continued weapon readiness and the gun controller in the operations room aimed and fired the weapon. The gun had a rate of fire of about 25 rounds per minute and a range of 12 nautical miles (22 km or 27.5 km with the newer high-explosive extended-

A good view of the Sea Dart launcher on HMS *Bristol*; the red missiles are dummies, usually loaded for show when the ship is in harbour. This launcher is the Mod 0 and was to be fitted to the CVA-01 carriers; in the end *Bristol* was the only ship to carry this version – a lighter and smaller version Mod 1 was fitted to the Type 42 (2) and Invincible-class carriers. (Rob Griffin)

range round). A particularly good video of this weapon taken from a camera inside the turret (not Bristol) during a firing exercise on one of the Type 42 destroyers, is available on YouTube and is well worth a view, just to see the speed the system works at.

The first recipient of the new gun and mount, the Mark 8, was the Iranian frigate *Zaal*, in 1971; the gun entered Royal Navy service in 1973 on HMS *Bristol*.

However, with all the automation involved, these guns proved to be less reliable than the older 4.5-inch Mark V gun (redesignated Mark VI gun mounting) during the Falklands War, being forced to cease fire on several occasions due to faults – shades of the

automated systems fitted to the Tiger-class cruisers: awesome to watch on film but a nightmare to maintain in an operational state.

As always with equipment as it was used and user feedback was considered, modifications followed on. The first major modification to the mounting was Mod 1, which was developed in 1998 and applied in two batches; it replaced the fibreglass cover with a reduced radar cross-section assembly, replacing the hydraulic loading mechanism with an all-electric system. Once this was done the look of the turret changed drastically: it was no longer a nice smooth shape, instead a series of faceted angles, which led to it being nicknamed' Kryten' by members of

A good frontal view showing the large size of the Mod 0 launcher for Sea Dart; the missile was effective during its operational use in the Falklands War and claimed several kills. (HMS *Bristol*)

Royal Navy, after the odd-shaped head of a robot from the British sci-fi comedy series *Red Dwarf*. Babcock upgraded 13 guns to Mod 1 standard between 2005 and 2012, and it is this version that is still in service on the Type 23 frigates today. They will be the last to probably carry this weapon as the new Type 26 frigates will be equipped with the new Mk 45 Mod 4 5-in/62-calibre gun, produced by BAE.

Located behind the 4.5 gun was the location of the Ikara anti-submarine missile system. The theory behind it was that it allowed a torpedo to be launched at a detected submarine very quickly, faster than the detecting vessel could cover the distance to the reported position, by which time the submarine had in all likelihood moved away, and so the hunt might have to start all over again. Today this is not a problem as helicopters carrying dipping sonar also carry anti-submarine missiles or depth charges; ships' helicopters similarly armed can be easily vectored onto the location; however, shipborne anti-submarine helicopters were still a new idea when Ikara was developed.

Ikara was named after the Aboriginal word for throwing stick, which seemed quite apt. The Ikara was a 'rocket-thrown-weapon' with some similarities to the French Malafon. It differed from the Malafon in that the torpedo was semi-recessed in the missile body rather than mounted in the nose. Ikara's range of

The rear of a Sea Dart launcher. On the deck behind it can just be made out the rails along which the resupply of missiles would be pushed until the missile could be taken onto the launcher in a reverse loading sequence taking the missile to the magazine. Today these rails are all that are left of the system. (HMS *Bristol*)

10 nautical miles (19 km) was double that of the ASROC (Anti-Submarine Rocket). Ikara was generally considered a superior system to the ASROC as it was accurately guided during flight to ensure optimal targeting. Its big advantage from a conventional type of attack, was the submarine would be aware from sonar contacts that it was about to be attacked and could engage in evasive changes of course. In ASROC's flight time to maximum range of 55 seconds, a submarine travelling at 25 knots (46 km/h) could move 700 metres (2,300 feet) from its position at launch, and a prediction would be made of the submarine's likely position at torpedo splashdown. But during the design of Ikara around 1960, the range of the acoustic

seeker of the Mk 44 torpedo was limited to 457 metres (1,499 feet), and consequently its kill probability was low. The range of the acoustic seeker was later improved.

Ikara was powered by a two-stage in-line solid-fuel Murawa rocket engine developed by Bristol Aerojet Ltd in the UK and was guided by radio command link until it reached the vicinity of the submarine, determined by the ship's sonar contact, where it would first jettison the rear ventral fin and torpedo rear covering and then release its 12.7-inch Mark 44 or Mark 46 acoustically guided anti-submarine torpedo.

The torpedo payload would descend by parachute while the missile itself

1973

Commissioned - Saturday 31st March

Amsterdam
Bristol

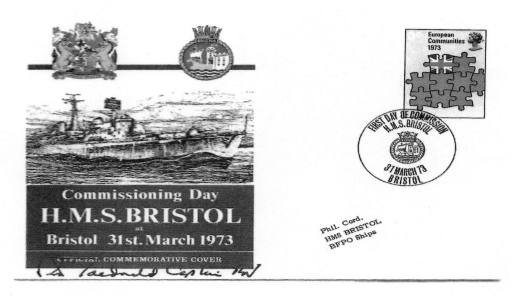

The beginning of it all, commissioning day, which is an event highly regarded in the Royal Navy. *Bristol* was unique in that she was at, or as near as possible to, the city she was named after, which at the time was a first. (HMS *Bristol*)

was programmed to splash down some distance away to avoid interference with the acoustic torpedo's seeker head. The torpedo would then begin a circular search pattern to find and lock onto a submarine contact and hopefully destroy it. One wonders if the recipients of this mode of attack would have been taken by surprise as was intended.

As for its use on HMS *Bristol*, it always created a good audience of Goofers (Royal Navy slang or Jackspeak for those with nothing to do, or spectators); however, the result of firing a rocket engine in a recessed launch area such as the 'pit' on *Bristol* meant that the whole area was covered in soot and the paintwork burnt off, and, as you can guess, it all had to made shipshape again.

Thus, the firing of a single shot was not the most popular event.

Bernard Campbell recalls the use of Ikara on *Bristol*:

> I fired it a few times between 1977 and 1980. Only problem was the mess it made of the launcher area burnt all the paint off and total repaint job, but it flew well and worked as far as I can remember. We had a firing in '79/'80. Everyone was on the flight deck, and they shot it straight over the bows so all we saw was a cloud of smoke after a loud whoosh.

Philip Cooter too recalls:

> The time is 1980 or 1981 in the Gib [Gibraltar] exercise area. We fired an Ikara exercise with its safety/arming plug in. It went for miles and

Although not HMS *Bristol*'s launcher, it is a good image that captures the mess that is created by missile firing. The Mod 1 launcher differences can be seen and the flash doors through which the missiles travel onto the launcher can be clearly seen under the launcher arms. (HMS *Exeter*)

miles. I opened the stowage box and there were these little green plugs (safety) and one yellow (arming). I told DWEO [Deputy Weapons Engineering Officer Peter Marsden, now a published author] and he said, 'I won't tell anyone if you don't.' Probably saved a court martial.

With the development of nuclear power, submarine performance, especially speed, improved dramatically, as did the threat they posed. Simultaneously, sonar-detection capability at long range was also improving significantly, so the Limbo mortar was developed to try and counter the threat. It was

Although this is HMS *Andromeda*, a Leander-class frigate, it does show the launch tubes of the Corvus system; this is obviously either Navy Day or a ship's family day as can be evidenced by the civilian figures. Afterwards, the Falklands ships were fitted with the SRBOC launcher to supplement the Corvus system. (HMS *Andromeda*)

Looking down into the Sea Dart magazine rear, the missiles were stored on the bases that can be seen and were moved to the launch rails by the controller who was located high up on the starboard side in a control room, looking down on the missiles from a window. From there he could select the type of missile to be loaded. *Bristol* had the largest magazine of any of the Sea Dart-equipped ships. (HMS *Bristol*)

located at the stern in its own well, which was also the location on other ships that eventually were equipped with it. The Limbo, or to give it its correct name, Anti-Submarine Mortar Mark 10, was the final British development of a forward-throwing anti-submarine weapon originally designed during the Second World War. Limbo, a three-barrelled mortar similar to the earlier Hedgehog and Squid which it superseded, was developed by the Admiralty Underwater Weapons Establishment in the 1950s. Unlike its predecessors though, its mounting was stabilised in pitch and roll, which it was hoped would improve its accuracy. The Squid was loaded manually, which was difficult on a pitching deck in heavy seas with no protection from the elements; in contrast, Limbo was loaded and fired automatically, with all the crew under cover. It was commonly installed on the quarterdeck of Royal Navy escort ships from 1955 to the mid-1980s. Australian–built versions of the Daring-class destroyer all carried Limbo as did the Australian River-class destroyer

Looking towards the launch rail system in the Sea Dart magazine, the actual launch rail hoist can just be seen to the left of the left-hand missile. (HMS *Bristol*)

The SRBOC launcher that was fitted to supplement the original Corvus chaff launchers after the Falklands. (Wikimedia Commons)

escort. Limbo was also widely employed by the Royal Canadian Navy, being incorporated into all destroyer designs from the late 1950s to the early 1970s, including the St Laurent, Restigouche, Mackenzie, Annapolis, and Iroquois classes. Limbo was carried on the Type 12 President-class frigates built for the South African Navy in the 1960s.

The firing distance of the mortars was controlled by opening gas vents; rounds could be fired from 400–1,000 yards (370–910 metres). The weapon was linked to the sonar system of the ship, firing on command when the target was in range. The rounds were projected so that they fell in a triangular pattern around the target. Limbo could fire in any direction around the ship and is reported to have been very accurate. The weapon was used in the 1982 Falklands War and remained in service in the Royal Navy and Commonwealth navies until the 1990s. A surviving system is preserved at Explosion, the Museum of Naval Firepower, in Gosport, Hampshire. After the 1976-7 refit, amongst other things, the Limbo mortar was removed, but as mentioned earlier it lurked in its own pit, so what was that to be utilised for? It could have been simply plated over, or maybe have improved the limited flying area, but no! the Commanding Officer came up with the solution in the best traditions of the Royal Navy: turn it into a swimming pool, and that's exactly what happened, and it remained so until it had to be plated over prior to her deployment to the South Atlantic. The expressions from any United States Navy

The Malkara missile with the torpedo that it carried, which can be seen just below the nose. The system was an Australian-developed anti-submarine weapon. (Rob Griffin)

With a sheet of flame and lots of smoke, the Malkara anti-submarine missile is launched from its lair, causing a large amount of cleaning to be carried out. The missile will travel towards the submarine contact and at a predetermined point the missile releases the underslung torpedo which then proceeds to hunt for the target; the missile will carry on and eventually land in the sea. (HMS Bristol Association)

The twin 30-mm automatic mounting fitted to *Bristol* and to other ships as a result of experience gained from the Falklands War; it is operated by a gunner who sits on the right side and is a fully powered system. (Wikimedia Commons)

The old but still-useful 20-mm Oerlikon cannon. This is a vintage mounting compared to the latest variant; this made up a third of the weapons mounted on *Bristol*'s gun deck. (Wikimedia Commons)

Another weapon system fitted as a result of experience gained from the Falklands War was this 20-mm Oerlikon cannon, which is a belt-fed manually controlled weapon; two were fitted to *Bristol*, one either side, along with the 30-mm mounting. (Wikimedia Commons)

personnel who were invited to a 'pool party' on board must have been worth seeing, especially when jack [sailor] would say, 'Oh, don't you have swimming pools on your ships then?'

Staying at the stern of the ship, we have the Sea Dart surface-to-air missile system, which again was a first for HMS *Bristol*; the system in its Mod 1 version went on to be fitted to all Type 42 destroyers plus the two that the UK sold to Argentina and all three of the Invincible-class light carriers.

The Sea Dart was a two-stage, 4.4-metre (14-feet)-long missile weighing 550 kilograms (1,210 lb). It is launched using a drop-off Chow solid-fuel booster that accelerates it to the supersonic speed necessary for the operation of the cruise motor, a Rolls-Royce kerosene-fuelled Odin ramjet. This gives a cruise speed of over Mach 2.5, and unlike many rocket-powered designs, the cruise engine burns for the entire flight, giving excellent terminal manoeuvrability at extreme range. It is capable of engaging

targets out to at least 30 nautical miles (35 mi, 56 km) over a wide range of altitudes. It has a secondary capability against small surface vessels, tested against a Brave-class patrol boat, although in surface mode the warhead safety arming unit does not arm and thus damage inflicted is restricted to the physical impact of the half-ton missile body and the unspent proportion of the 46 litres (10 imp gal, 12 US gal) of kerosene fuel.

Guidance is by proportional navigation and a semi-active radar homing system using the nose intake cone and four aerials around the intake as an interferometer aerial, with targets being identified by Type 1022 surveillance radar (originally radar Type 965) and illuminated by one of a pair of radar Types 909. This allows two targets to be engaged simultaneously in initial versions, with later variants (see below) able to engage more. Firing is from a twin-arm trainable launcher that is loaded automatically from below decks. The Sea Dart magazine had the

The venerable 20-mm Oerlikon being fired from HMS *Bristol*. Note the drum-type magazine on the top right of the weapon and the spent 20-mm cases on the deck. (Phil Langois)

The fun of firing the 20-mm Oerlikon cannon. The gunner is held in place by the supports over his shoulders; the ammunition feed can be seen to the right of the gun, although this particular weapon is fitted to a T42 destroyer. The effect would be very much the same on *Bristol*.

The underside of the 4.5-inch gun. When this is in action the loading, firing, and ejecting of the empty case turns into a blur. The turret is only a light fibreglass moulding and is designed to protect the system from the elements as there are no crew inside when the turret is at action. (HMS *Exeter*)

largest magazine capacity of any of the Sea Dart-equipped warships; the missiles were stored on a moving conveyor that allowed the controller to select the correct missile – he had a window overlooking the magazine, and that and his control area are still there today. The magazine itself had been converted to a lecture theatre, which was very cleverly done. It had cinema-type seats arranged on a slope, but the area where the lectern and screen were still had the missile loading gear visible, as well as lots of markings around the theatre to remind one what it was once like.

The original launcher seen on the *Bristol* was significantly larger than that which appeared on the Type 42 and Invincible classes. Initial difficulties with launcher reliability and missile performance were mostly ironed out by the trials carried out by *Bristol*, although no system is 100 per cent reliable and there are several horror tales of the 'the day it went wrong', including again a video on YouTube that catches all the drama of a Sea Dart launch – apart from the fact that after the launch the motor fell off and lay on the deck burning while the rest of the missile fell overboard (again, not on Bristol).

Sea Dart was used in anger during the Falklands War and had eight confirmed successful engagements in combat, including six aircraft, a helicopter, and an anti-ship missile. However, an additional helicopter was shot down in a 'friendly fire' incident, killing all on board. A few suspicious clouds were also engaged along with a missile fired at the Argentine Boeing 707 reconnaissance aircraft: although no hit was registered, the aircraft was forced to veer away. The launcher was removed during her conversion and the area became the sewage treatment plant. The only visible sign of the system are the rails on the deck above the sewage plant that were used for loading replenishment missiles; the radar fibreglass domes are still there but are simply empty covers and serve as nothing more exciting than being used to store items that need to be out of sight.

George Darroch relates some Sea Dart woes:

Steve 'Baz' Barry was on the flight deck when two rounds appeared on the launcher unexpectedly. I remember that day very well! As part of the flight deck crew at action stations, I had spent many an hour in 'peace time' with the rest of the flight deck crew sitting against the guardrails with cigarette on the go; however, this time the launcher makes a move, nothing is announced on ship's Tannoy, doors open and two white missiles yellow banded are loaded then the whole thing moves and points to the horizon. Shiiiiittttt! Arms up, we run like f*** and get inside, slam the watertight door, and manage to get the first clip on when, whoosh, whoosh and they are airborne. When we were stood down the flight deck crew go onto the flight deck. The guardrails me and fellow crew were leaning on are gone and the Joss's [Master at Arms] flight deck comms lead and box are a melted blob on the deck.

The moment a Sea Dart missile comes up from the magazine and starts loading onto the launch rails. Notice the blast door is in the down position; once the missile is clear it will close. (HMS *Bristol*)

HMS *Bristol* carried two sonars, one in a fixed dome, and one with a dome that could be retracted; this not-often-seen view is of the retractable one taken looking aft. (HMS *Bristol*)

This shows the second fixed sonar dome. It is also obvious from the picture that a special requirement when the ship is dry-docked is to ensure that the domes are not damaged as they protrude below the keel line. (HMS *Bristol*)

A couple of malfunction bits that occurred with Sea Dart, these being more the rarity than the normal. A Sea Dart missile was cut in two when the lower flash door malfunctioned and closed on a missile separating the boost motor from the sustainer motor and scattered bits of missile around the intermediate hoist and the magazine – 1981 if I remember correctly. Bill Backshell was the handling system maintainer, and I was the firing system maintainer. Brum Waterson will clearly remember going under the rails to find every small bit of the missile that was distributed around the magazine. Quite a moment! Another incident occurred at a similar time when embarking Sea Dart missiles from the embarkation container by the launcher. There, a hydraulic hose burst, covering the rear end of the ship in oil at 3,000 psi. The missile canister dropped some distance and, guess what, broke another missile in two. That said, the missile system was actively used in the Falklands in 1982 and never once let us down operationally. It was a fantastic system. In my time there were some really excellent maintainers including Jan Coles, Bill Backs hell and Brock Booster. I was relieved in 1983 by Ian Maconie.

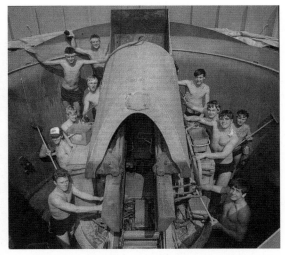

Smiles for the camera but out of shot I suspect is a lot of muttering going on, as it appears they are just about finishing cleaning the Malkara pit after a launch. (Steve A. Wenham)

Her weapons fit as described, changed over the years and especially after the Falklands, although the first additions were fitted around 1979, approximately two years after her major refit after the fire in the steam turbine room, when she received two Corvus chaff launchers and also a UAA-1 electronic upgrade on her mainmast. After her return from the Falklands, she, like most of the fleet, landed her ship's boats and had extra small arms added to increase close-range firepower. For *Bristol* this meant the addition of two BMARC/Oerlikon twin 30-mm mounts and two single GAMB01 20-mm mounts, which, along with her original aged 20-mm single-mount Oerlikon, were mounted on a gun deck.

As built, she was intended to be fitted with the Anglo-Dutch Type 988 3D radar mounted in an exceptionally large dome on her forward mast; the same as was to be fitted to the new carriers, in the end this was not fitted and instead she received what was then the Royal Navy standard radar, the Type

HMS *Bristol* carried two sonars, one in a fixed dome, and one with a dome that could be retracted; this not-often-seen view is of the retractable one taken looking aft. (HMS *Bristol*)

This view show Bristol's Type 1022 radar on the foremast, which was classed as a search and range finder radar; it replaced the old 'bedstead' Type 965 system. Looks as though 'A look at the Navy' briefing is going on. (HMS *Bristol*)

Almost an identical view to the previous image, but this time a much earlier time frame, located on the foremast, is the Type 965 'bedstead' radar; this was used to give long-range aircraft warnings. (HMS *Bristol*)

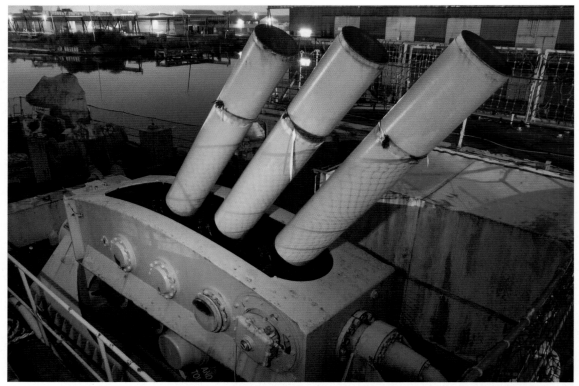

The Limbo mortar located in what would become *Bristol*'s swimming pool! This was the final development of mortars developed during the war to combat the U-boat threat. When fired it had a range of 400–1,000 feet (370–910 metres); it was fired in anger during the Falklands and was controlled by one of the sonar systems, which would indicate when the target was in range. (Tom Blackwell)

965 air search radar AKE-2, which could be either a single or double and was known as the 'bedstead' radar. She also had a Type 992Q low-angle search radar, two Type 909 Sea Dart target illumination radars (under the large GRP domes fore and aft) and a Type 978 navigation radar.

For sonar detection she was built for two types, one being the Type 170 search sonar and the other being Type 184 target indication set. These were housed in two separate domes near the bow; one was fixed while the other could be raised into the hull.

Her big step forward in ship electronics was the fitting of the ADAWS-2 (Action Data Automation Weapons System Mk 2), a computer system designed to coordinate the ship's weapons and sensors, which was a great leap forward from the County-class destroyers in service at the time as they relied heavily on manual input data, The system was based on two F1600 computers manufactured by Ferranti, which would accept data from all of the ship's sensors and automatically produce a track for each target and list them in order of importance before engaging with the appropriate weapon system. Today this sort of procedure is almost taken for granted but back then it was ground-breaking technology. During the refit when the weapons were upgraded, she also received the more modern Type 1022 radar to replace the old double 'bedstead'; she was also rumoured to be fitted with the Phalanx close-in weapon system (CIWS): although she was never fitted with the system, it seems she was fitted *for* but not *with*, which means that if she had

The twin 30-mm in action on the gun deck; notice the single gunner employed and the fact that other personnel are keeping well clear. Notice too the net rails are in the lowered position to allow firing; when the weapon is not in use, they will be raised to the vertical position very much like the nets around flight decks. (Tudor Weeks)

to go to war again, the system could have been installed with minimum fuss.

Although not a weapon, this seems the ideal place to mention them. She was fitted with two types of sonar, the Type 184M and the Type182. She also carried for self-defence Corvus chaff launchers and later on was fitted with modified SBROC (Super Rapid-Blooming Off-board) chaff launchers.

With all the equipment fitted she was at one time the most powerful warship in the Royal Navy and most certainly had the most advanced command and communications platform in the navy.

One constant, amusing, fact is although she was permanently moored at Whale Island, Portsmouth, serving out her days as harbour training and accommodation ship, if you took the harbour tour you would see her, but listening carefully to the commentary that could be quite amusing. For instance, she was the last warship in the Royal Navy to have three funnels, that is one funnel for each engine – bit of a problem when she had four. Recently we were told that she had been stripped of all machinery and was nothing but an empty hull, which used the vacant spaces to create dormitories and classrooms (again, not exactly spot-on information).

So, there we have the background to the only Type 82, HMS *Bristol*, and now we have her afloat and fully equipped, ready to go, before we look at how the Royal Navy actually employed her and her many roles through her long life. Let us take a quick tour of the ship, visiting many areas as they were recently and try to visualise her as she was.

A SHIP'S TOUR

This a view from the port side of HQ1 looking forward. Just visible is the circular blanking plate where once the 4.5-inch turret was mounted; forward of that can be seen the anchor winch controls with their control wheels painted red and green to represent port and starboard respectively. (Rob Griffin)

We begin our tour at Whale Island, home to HMS *Excellent* shore base establishment, and the location of HMS *Bristol*'s permanent home since she was decommissioned as an active warship, before being recommissioned as the harbour training and accommodation ship. Before we start, just what does that role actually mean? As a training ship, she serves an important purpose in allowing various branches of the RN to be able to use her to help with their training, the facilities she has to offer are always available and it also means that an operational warship is not tied up being used for the role. An example of the type of training would be for marine engineers, who will get their first taste of how cramped engineering spaces can be, although modern warships are better in that aspect, but the training is worthwhile. They also will be shown the problems involved in moving large unwieldly objects in very cramped spaces, as we shall see in later images. A visit to any of the engineering spaces will show the amount of work that is put in by the trainees; during a visit I was shown all the marker pen lines and writing on the various pipe runs as the trainees were tasked to trace flow patterns. Another advantage is that it is relatively safer on her as the boilers and engine spaces are no longer used so Health & Safety are happy.

Anther use is training for the divers who use the hull to hone their skills or to learn them and at times the ship can resonate to the sound of gunfire, but nothing to worry about, as it is only periodic exercises carried out on by the RN and Royal Marines. In her role as an accommodation ship, she is invaluable: for the RN there just is not enough accommodation to cover courses, visitors and those working in the Portsmouth area, so she is of immense aid in resolving that problem – even so, the dockyard is often bursting at the seams. Finally, she is used by the cadet forces and obviously the Sea Cadets are the biggest users, but the other two services also make use of her. It gives young people a fantastic chance to live on board a warship for a few nights and for those thinking of joining the navy

One of the entrances to the ship's internals from 1 deck; many of these access doors now have signs telling you for adults only or ship's company only or no cadets. (Rob Griffin)

The commanding officer's office and a very small one it is, chock a block with documents, books, computer and the best model of the ship on board. From here the CO will control the day-to-dayrunning of the ship, which can be especially busy when a full load of cadets is aboard. (Rob Griffin)

The signal deck looking rather new; this view is looking starboard. Note the speakers and various boxes located on the wings; also on the right a Stevenson's screen weather box. (HMS *Bristol*)

this presents a realistic impression of what they will encounter. The accommodation is basic, with cadets separated into male and female accommodation; there are the normal ablutions and heads, a quiet room, and various games spaces. If more than one group is on board new friendships are very quickly formed and, in some cases, last a lifetime. I recently took a group of cadets for a weekend on board, and as we headed home their first question was, 'Can we do it again?' In that role she is invaluable.

We approach the ship along a bridge that leads to the pontoons alongside her starboard side where various small craft are tied up on one side; these are used by the RN to teach sailing and powerboating skills, but the visitor's eye is immediately drawn to the bulk of HMS

Bristol which might not seem much compared to something like HMS *Queen Elizabeth* aircraft carrier, but for those who have never served the description of a destroyer leads to impression that they are small ships. Standing at the start of the pontoons alongside her, one cannot help but be impressed at the size; also, it is not very often that a warship is viewed from such a low angle, all of which adds to the impression of size.

We board her by a series of fixed steps of which there are two sets, one forward used for day-to-day use and for visitors, the other aft and are mainly for the permanent crew's use. Boarding her in this fashion is vastly different to the brow that those who served will recall; the steps are adorned with safety information for the visitor.

Part of the wardroom dining area, which still retains its well-looked-after image even though formal meals are a thing of the past. (Rob Griffin)

Once at the top, the visitor is now at 1 deck. Directly in front is the lifebelt mounted on a stand bearing the ship's name, and if the visitor were to look down, they would see the brass plate with BRISTOL on it let into the deck. If it is a service visitor and they were in uniform they would salute, providing the Union Jack and White Ensign are flying, if not then a respectful pause before setting foot on board is the norm.

For ordinary visitors the first stop will be the entrance to HQ1 just to the right of the lifebelt. In an operational warship, HQ1 is located several decks down and it is from there that the damage control of the ship is managed; however, the HQ1 we are about to enter is responsible for the security of the ship and all visitors, regardless of who they are. They will advise the duty QM (Quarter Master) who is normally a member of the civilian staff employed on the ship: details on who you are and who you wish to meet

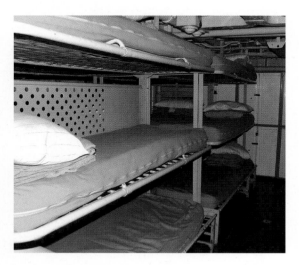

A typical mess deck sleeping area today. Because of her size the mess areas were quite generous compared to other ships, but still not spacious. Today it is fun watching the cadets when confronted with duvets and covers that have to be fitted by themselves and not a sign of mum to do it. (Rob Griffin)

This is the SCC, on 3 deck. It is from the SCC that all machinery from propulsion to sewage is controlled by a team of marine engineers who are likely to man the compartment 24 hours a day, every day, until she decommissions. Also located in here is the emergency steering position. (Rob Griffin)

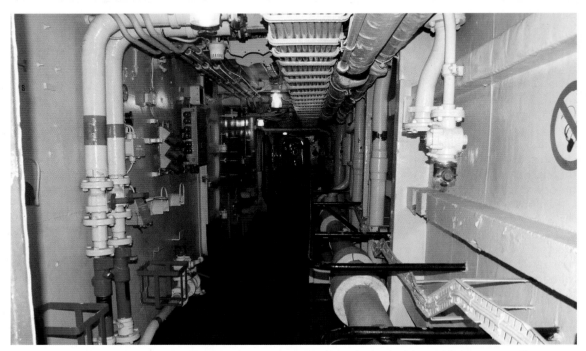

The view along this corridor shows just how much space is taken up by pipes and cables and fittings. Notice the now-empty fire hose reels; firefighting and equipment are top priority in a warship. (Rob Griffin)

The Sea Dart theatre, showing the excellent job of converting the magazine to a first-class theatre; the missile hoist can be seen in the far distance, and much of the original fittings are still there but now hidden under the sloping floor. (Rob Griffin)

are recorded and then, if necessary, the host for that person will be traditionally piped on the ship's Tannoy system, and, depending on your status, you might, once booked in, be allowed to tour on your own.

We now can commence our tour of the ship. Coming out of HQ1 and facing the starboard side, we turn left and head to the bows. Once we are there, we can see that the layout of the anchoring facilities has not changed that much, if at all, since she was launched., Bristol carries two anchors, one each port and starboard. The chains and capstans and controls are still there, although it is a long time since they were used, but they are still maintained and look as though they could be used instantly. In fact, if you look over the starboard side

This shows the mounting frame for one of the gas turbine units, long removed from the ship, and sadly an air of neglect does seem to be evident; these are areas that are rarely visited and not usually by visitors. (Rob Griffin)

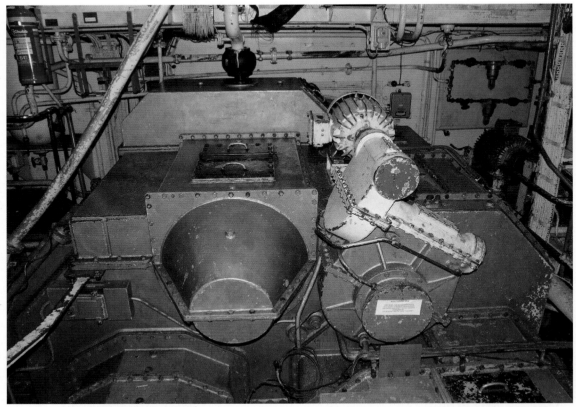

This is one of the two gearboxes fitted to *Bristol* but the image does not give an indication as to how large they are; before entering the gearbox spaces there is a contraband box into which all non-essential items are placed, which was to prevent something that was not needed accidentally being left in the gearbox, as the damage caused by something simple as a spanner could be horrendous. (Rob Griffin)

This is all that is left of the machinery that once operated one of the stabilisers; the hydraulic ram can clearly be see seen in the centre. It was hoped that stabilisers when in use would help limit the movement during rough weather. (Rob Griffin)

of the ship you will see the permanent mooring arrangements in use. There are two stations arranged in a triangle and onto these is fitted a sliding connector, which is bolted to the ship's side foreword and aft: as the tide goes out, they allow her to settle lower down and when the tide comes in the process is reversed – a very simple but efficient system that saves having to adjust moorings all the time.

Moving back past the breakwater, we are greeted by a large circular metal plate bolted to the deck. This is the area where the 4.5 turret was once located and if we were to follow this through the various decks to the magazine, all that would be visible are the side walls of the trunking and a few warning notices. Unlike when HMS *Kent* was in a

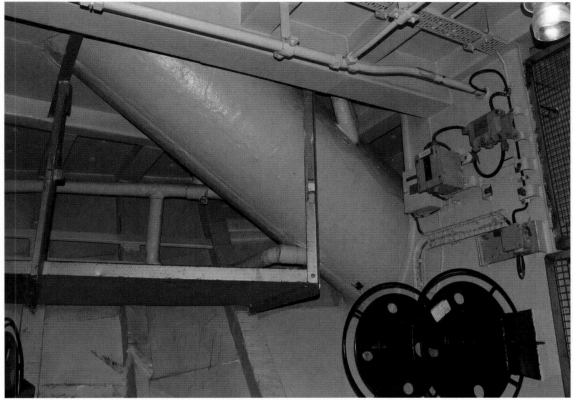

This is the fore peak (near the stem) of the ship. Running across the shot is the hawse pipe through which the anchor chain runs; notice the now-empty cable reels on the right and in the distance. (Rob Griffin)

similar role and kept her turrets and most of her fittings, sadly *Bristol* has lost much of her original outline

Further back we come to the storage area that once housed the ship's motor vehicle, which mostly was a SWB Land Rover. Today it is used for storage. Inside there is access down to 2 deck. When in service, there were two sitcom antennae located on the top of the area, but these like many other fittings have been removed. Moving back, we come to an open area of deck space, and this is where the Ikara lurked in its pit: no trace can be seen of it now, which to many is a good thing, considering the work involved in cleaning it after firing. If we turn and face the stern, we have a good view of the bridge frontal area. Mounted on top of the area that we met as HQ1 is the fibreglass dome that used to cover and protect the forward 909 Sea Dart radar tracker – now it is just an empty dome;

Located on the bridge, the inclinometer is a really 'hi-tec' piece of equipment as can be seen in the image. It was nothing more than a pivoted pointer and a graduated scale and although simple in construction it worked; it showed the inclination of the ship when she was heeling or if damaged how far she was listing. (Rob Griffin)

A view looking up from the forward mast with its twin 965 radar on top. This is often referred to as the 'bedstead' radar due to its slight resemblance to a bedstead. This would be replaced after the Falklands War with the more modern Type 1022 radar with a much lower profile. (HMS *Bristol*)

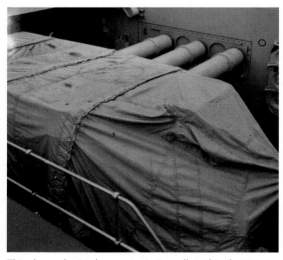

This shows the Limbo mortar in its well; in this shot it is in the horizontal position and fitted with a canvas cover to protect it from the elements. Limbo was the last in a long line of projectors developed from the Second World War. (HMS *Bristol*)

it is surprising just how tall it is, but it does not interfere with the view from the bridge.

Moving astern along the starboard side, we pass under the deck that originally held life raft containers but later had the SBROC chaff launchers fitted; these were similar to the Corvus launchers already installed but they had a better blooming effect once deployed. The support for it contains the 'T' board that is used to indicate whether personnel are aboard or onshore; this would be used to determine numbers in the event of a fire. Moving further aft we pass under the gun deck, which was built out from 1 deck; this was added after the Falklands War, and it supported the three weapons systems that we have already discussed. Along both sides of this superstructure are three typical RN doors with the handles for clipping the door securely closed; due to the role that *Bristol* now plays some are marked with signs that

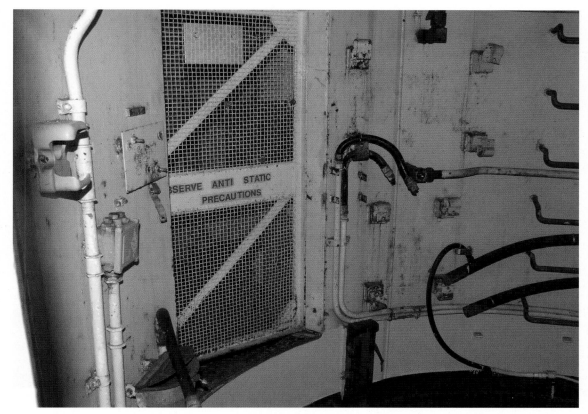

A very empty area that once was part of the 4.5-inch gun mounting; note the warning sign on the access door on the left, now used as a storage area. (Rob Griffin)

would never have been seen in her active days. This is to ensure that only the correct personnel use the correct entrance, some marked for crew use, others no cadets, which does not always work if you have hyperactive young people aboard.

We will take the first door that we come to which has a wooden inner door marked in gold lettering, 'Officers Only', which I suspect is a reminder of her service days. Below that a red plate is marked 'Adults Only No Youth Groups', the reason why is apparent once we enter. As we walk forward, we see on our left the closed door marked 'Commanding Officer', hence why no youth groups. To our front right is a small galley and to our immediate right is a single head and next to it is the wardroom with its bar. The ship's battle honours board is also mounted on a bulkhead in this area. Moving forward we can

see some of the officers' original cabins, still in use today. As we move on, we come to a set of quite steep ladders with a sign pointing up to the bridge; we climb these and come out on 1 deck where another set of steps leads us to the bridge itself. Before looking around, now that we have climbed both sets of ladders, the following tale might be more appreciated: Adam 'Ski' Whitehead recalls:

This is an incident that happened whilst on passage up the Thames to Greenwich in '83. It was early in the morning, about 0430, special sea duty men closed up and the ship in 2 Yankee [ship in darkened condition, only essential lights on] when the navigator phoned down from the bridge asking for two cups of coffee and two rounds of bacon butties for the OOW [Officer Of the Watch] and himself. This request was dutifully carried out and a young

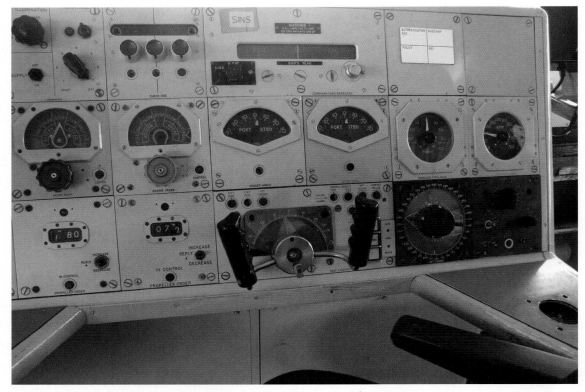

Any image the reader may have developed from TV movies and the like of a steadfast sailor clutching a large ship's wheel will sadly be shattered by this image as the steering controls look more like something from a video game, however much easier to use and less tiring on those using it; all the information is available on the dials in front. This is located in the bridge on 3 deck. (Rob Griffin)

STWD [steward] was sent to the bridge with aforementioned victuals. Ten or 15 mins later he returns to the wardroom with a full tray! Puzzled, I asked the young lad if the navigator had changed his mind. 'No,' he said. 'So why do you still have a full tray?' I asked, 'There's nobody up there,' he replied. 'What do mean there's nobody up there?' I asked. His reply almost brought me to tears: 'All the lights are off, there's no one up there.' Nice one.

I am sure we have all done something similar and felt very silly at the end of it. We now can move into the actual bridge area and probably find it surprisingly cramped to what we may have expected. The one comment that is always heard is, 'Where is the steering wheel?' When the small aircraft-type control is pointed out, most visitors are a bit stunned. This is located centrally and besides the steering controls, there are numerous gauges, so that most of the functions needed to control the ship are at hand. The view from the bridge is very good and due to its height not really affected by the 909 Radar dome below. There are various radar screens and chart tables around the bridge, but it would still be cramped with all the duty watch in place.

We can leave the bridge and walk out onto the wings and view the signal flag lockers that would have held all the flags that the signals team used; the large signal lamps would have been located here too but they have also been removed. While outside we can look around and just behind are the support platforms where the SCOT (satellite communications on board terminal) domes were located. Then looking over the side we can look down onto the area where the

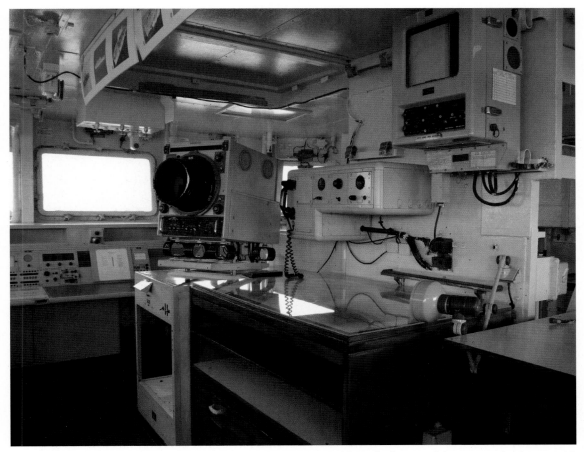

This part of the bridge contains the chart table that the navigator would use; further round the area are the drawers with all the charts he would hopefully need; near the tab are the various electronic aids such as a radar repeater. (Rob Griffin)

catwalk is, the area that held the T board and originally life raft containers plus an Oerlikon 20-mm cannon. These were later removed and SBROC launchers fitted; the Oerlikon was moved onto the new gun deck.

Looking forward, to the remains of the foremast which is located to the rear of the bridge structure; when she first took up her new role, this still stood at its full height complete with the radar, firstly the 1002 then that was replaced by the old 926 'bedstead'. However, as time went on and with a very much reduced crew, the upkeep was not what an operational warship would be kept at, and due to H&S issues it was felt the mast was becoming unsafe so was reduced in height and the radar went as well – the same

action was enacted on the main mast too. These alterations and removal of armament do raise comments from people such as: 'This is not the ship I served in' and yes, that is very true, but at least she is still here and doing a fantastic job, otherwise she would have been razor blades years ago.

Back inside the warmth of the bridge, it is pleasing to see that so much has been left as it was, although the traditional captain's chair is a very Spartan affair compared to those in use today.

One strange piece of equipment is the inclinometer, a very simple-looking instrument; in essence it is a triangle-shaped wooden board with a free-swinging pointer marked from zero to degrees port and

If nothing else the area shot to the left of the navigation table shows just how small a bridge *Bristol* had; almost circular in its layout, it could be crowded when all members of the watch were there. (Rob Griffin)

starboard, simple in concept, but it shows the angle of list.

We now reverse our way back down the stairs, making sure that we obey the signs telling us which way to face going down the

This is the rear of the bridge with the port access door visible; another such door was located on the starboard side and exiting this led onto the signal deck. (Rob Griffin)

ladders; this is completely irritating to those who have served as they are so used to doing the reverse of what the notices dictate, but that's H&S for you

Arriving safely back onto 1 deck, we now continue on our way. Aft we pass more cabins, and at this point it is worth stopping and taking a look inside: these are all officers' cabins and, depending on your rank would depend on the size of your cabin. The biggest one is just as we entered the area and I suspect that it was the Captain's or First Lieutenant's as it is by far the largest one aboard. The remainder, while sparse, do give the occupant more privacy and space than the mess decks lower in the ship. As we can see there is a single bunk, a washbasin and cupboard for toiletries and storage for personal belonging and uniforms: all this plus the added bonus of a sliding door to keep the rest of the world out when off duty. Notice the bottom of the door has a kickout panel, which would be used if

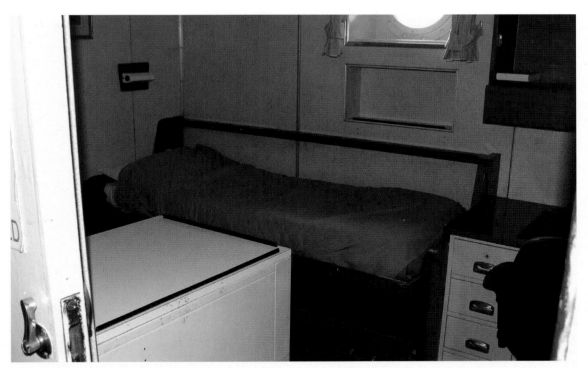

A typical single-berth officer's cabin. Even though it has more privacy than the mess decks, it is still compact; some were bigger such as the first lieutenant's and the captain's but otherwise this was standard. (Rob Griffin)

Although a slightly grainy image, it shows HMS *Bristol* having her 4.5-inch turret replaced; the old and the new turrets are visible. (Portsmouth Historical Dockyard)

This is the view visitors get when approaching HMS *Bristol*. The large triangular-shaped units are what actually secure her to her mooring place. (Rob Griffin)

for some reason the ship was in danger and the door could not be opened. As we move down the corridor, we can see various signs denoting whose area this is, such as officers' showers or officers' heads. What ex-members will find strange is the number of signs indicating female areas such as ablutions, heads (toilets) and accommodation. These were additions designed to cater for the ship's role as harbour accommodation ship and the influx of youth groups comprised of both males and females.

Moving further aft we come to a lobby with access port and starboard. If we turn to look forward, we will see a varnished board on the bulkhead, which gives details of the ship as launched. Turning to the stern we have what is now the is now the First Lieutenant's office, but originally it was part of the boiler uptakes. Looking closely at the bulkhead we can actually see a reminder of the amount of heat generated by the fire all those years ago, where it buckled the metal. The central feature here is the clipped open hatch that leads down to 2 deck, where the main accommodation is for the cadets. Some of it still will be recognisable to those who served or if you ever used one of those areas while on a course. Plenty of signs remain to show who the previous occupants were. The other item in this lobby is one of several models depicting HMS *Bristol*; the best one, surprisingly enough, is actually located in CO's office. The models vary in the standard of depiction of the ship, but generally give an overall top view of what she looked like in her service days. Keeping to the starboard side we move further aft, passing the duty

These daunting steps are the access to HMS *Bristol* these days, and they can be quite a challenge if you are coming aboard to stay, as getting your suitcase up is a struggle. (Rob Griffin)

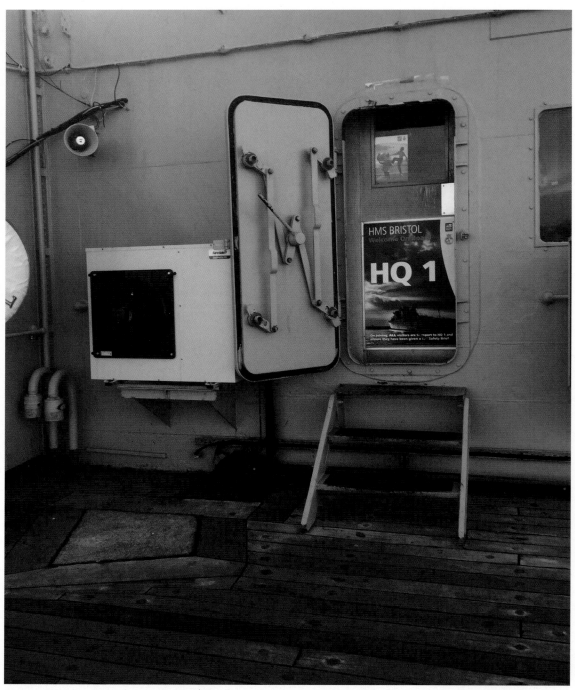

Having arrived on board ship you are greeted with the sign on the door saying HQ1, which is where all visitors must report before going anywhere else: inside the staff will verify who you are and, if necessary, pipe for your host to come and collect you. If you are staying on board one of the duty crew will escort you to your mess/cabin. You will also be given various safety briefs and issued with your T card, which you use when boarding/leaving the ship; this is system to help determine who is on board in the case of an emergency. (Rob Griffin)

A close-up of how the mooring system works. This is also in use in other locations in the dockyard at Portsmouth, notably on pontoons. (Rob Griffin)

hand's cabin and the technical officer's cabin at which point we take a sharp right followed by a sharp left and we have a cabinet to our right with trophies in it and on out left the noticeboard with the ship's daily orders and other information for the crew. Possibly of more interest to us, as by now we are probably feeling a little worn out, is what is now known as the Bristol Lounge, which is a lovely large space with comfortable chairs, a television and various books and games available. There is also a bar, which until recently meant we could get a nice glass of wine to relax with, but recent changes have decided it is not a good idea to have alcohol on board with cadets using the ship. So, the bar is no more of a tuck shop, but at least we

A corner of the wardroom, with the stairs leading to more officers' accommodation. The unit to the left front is where papers and periodicals would have been located for light reading. (Rob Griffin)

This corridor is located on 1 deck and the sign on the door at the far end reads, 'Quiet please duty personnel sleeping'. This is where the duty leading hand would sleep while on duty. (Rob Griffin)

can relax and have a cool soft drink while we take in our surroundings.

Where we are now used to be part of the wardroom and I am sure if the bulkheads could talk, we would hear some amazing tales. We also have a chance to see some of the Bristol-badged souvenirs that are available for purchase, which range from cap tallies to polo shirts, and are quite popular.

There is a doorway through which we can see a small spiral staircase, which is now only for use by the ship's crew but used to lead to more officers' accommodation. We now retrace our steps and find ourselves back on 1 deck, and moving further aft, we come to the end of the deck. We now overlook the flight deck/quarterdeck, where the most obvious feature in front of us is the large construction

If you were a cadet staying overnight, this is the first glimpse you will get of the access to your mess deck after leaving HQ1. You now have to get yourself and your kit through the hatch and down the ladder before making your way, thankfully, to your mess. It can be amusing to watch at times. (Rob Griffin)

If you were an adult staying aboard either on a course or looking after cadets, this was your little haven of peace: known as the Bristol Lounge, it had a bar, TV, newspapers, and magazines to help you unwind, plus a small galley by the entrance that provided self-service hot drinks. The sign above the bar is very telling. (Rob Griffin)

that totally fills the area originally occupied by the Sea Dart launcher. Inside this is the ship's sewage treatment plant, not as interesting as the launcher would have been but a very vital part of the ship. The only tangible remains of the Sea Dart launcher system if we stand directly behind the sewage plant and look down onto the deck, are two pairs of rails which were used when the reload missiles were loaded on board in their transit boxes when they would be laid horizontally on these rails and then removed and lowered onto the launcher rails and taken below to the Sea Dart magazine, in a reverse process of loading missiles to fire.

Either side are ladders that lead to the flight deck, which we descend carefully. The use of the phrase 'flight deck' does sometimes cause annoyance with some ex-crew members who feel that as it had no embedded helicopters then it's not a flight deck; but the fact is *Bristol* did host helicopters, of all sizes, although more for resupply or passing visits. Once safely down we can look forward and directly behind the sewage plant and see the large aft radar dome, which is identical to the one we saw forward on top of HQ1. Looking back, we can see that the superstructure tapers in toward where Sea Dart used to be, with an access door either side; these are the doors that the ship's crew used if caught unawares when a war load of Sea Dart missiles was loaded without warning.

One area that became a legend in its own lifetime can just about be made out on the deck: this of course is the famous swimming pool, constructed during the 1979 refit; this

Not the most salubrious of places but this is the onboard sewage treatment plant installed when the ship took on its current role. The plant occupies the space of the Sea Dart launcher and directly below it is the Sea Dart theatre. (Rob Griffin)

A close-up of the sliding shaft used in the fixed mooring system, a simple but excellent method of securing the ship alongside without the use of lines. (Rob Griffin)

was a novel feature and to this day I am still not sure how the captain got away with it as it certainly would not have been RN practice. All that is left now if you trace it carefully are the weld marks from the plates welded over the pool when *Bristol* was called up to the South Atlantic. It had to be plated over to allow her to operate helicopters, and the area below was then turned into a gym.

Looking aft, not much is left of the original fittings, and the deck is relatively uncluttered. During her operational days there was a winch and control box plus a rack for two dan buoys, used in minesweeping and centrally located, a large capstan – today, all that remains is the capstan. Located on the stern rail is the jack staff that supports the White Ensign; as *Bristol* is still a commissioned warship, the ceremony of Colours when the Union Flag and White

Located on the starboard side forward is the previously mentioned T board; each person on board has a T card and as can be seen these are in varying colours. If you are on board your card should be located in the in slot and if ashore located in the out slot: a very simple but effective way of monitoring who is where. (Rob Griffin)

Although a poor image, it shows the damage caused by the fire that destroyed the steam plant in 1974, but the value of steam and gas were proven when she ran for three years on gas turbines only. Today the results can be seen in a bulkhead near the XO's office that is still buckled from the heat of the fire. (Matthew Crofts)

Ensign are hoisted in the morning and evening Colours when they are lowered, should take place simultaneously on all ships in the harbour, with the senior one giving the signals by flags.

Having finished, we make our way back to the ladders and 1 deck. We take one of the sets of ladders that leads to 1 deck and climb to see what awaits us. The one part of 1 deck that is fairly obvious is the extension either side of it, which was added post-Falklands: this was built out so the smaller-arms weapons could be grouped together: so, you would have had looking from aft a modern 20-mm cannon, the twin 30-mm power mounting and the Second World War-vintage 20-mm Oerlikon cannon. The area that is covered by the 1 deck extension was the location for the ship's davits either side that carried the ships

boats, normally a pair of motor launches; once these were removed on *Bristol* and the same for the RN fleet, the only ship's boats were usually a pair of rigid inflatables, more commonly known as 'RIBs'.

Whilst on 1 deck we can climb into the platforms located port and starboard of the twin funnels; normally these would have had a pair of large signalling lamps fitted to them: now the only thing visible is the television aerial for the ship's crew. We move to the forward funnel that was used to vent the waste gases from the steam turbines; there is actually a small passageway that allows us to walk from side to side, before we reach the edge of the extension, where, looking forward, we can see a similar layout located near the current HQ1, which used to contain

Port gearbox and the high-pressure air compressor, and although not in use these machinery spaces are invaluable for training the engineers of tomorrow in working in confined spaces. It seems from the picture that even the army is in on the act. (Rob Griffin)

life raft storage, but again after the Falklands, they were moved and in their place was fitted the SUBROC launcher.

We now retrace our steps to the flight deck and this time we enter the superstructure via the starboard door. Located near this door is the crane that was used to lower the RIBs into the sea. Once we are in the warm again, we find ourselves in an open area. To our left is a wall with two large cut-outs into which the dirty linen is placed by visitors after their stay. This looks very efficient as it seems one lot of laundry is separated from another, but when you look at the rear of the wall, you will see no dividing wall, so everything gets mixed up: navy efficiency at its very best.

Moving along the companionway, we make our way forward through the ship, and take note of the various posters and

information notices along the way. Evidence of her changed role appears when just before we make a sharp turn left, we come across the civilian rest room near the area dedicated as cadets' recreational space, which contains table tennis and a television and seating: this is important as cadets are not allowed ashore on their own so entertainment has to be provided.

Further forward we have the various mess decks all labelled for males or females and similar for the heads and ablutions. Just before we come to the mess decks, on our left are some of the various offices that manage the ship's administration and bookings, both RN and cadets. On our right is the cadets' sick bay although for serious cases the civilian hospital will be utilised. Next to this is the duty Senior Rate cabin and duty male cabin:

The port rudder control arm in the steering flat; again, the size and thickness show well in the image, painted red and green for port and starboard. (Rob Griffin)

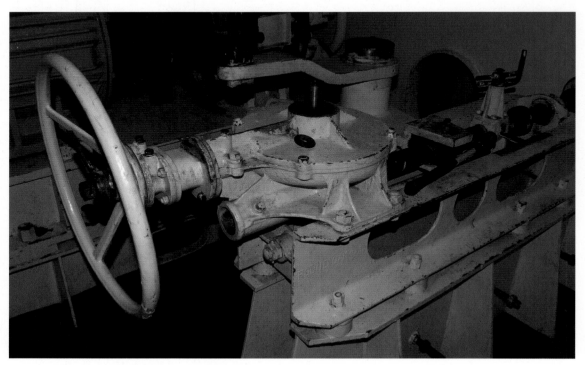

Located in the tiller flat is the last means of steering in an emergency: by turning the wheel the rudders can be operated but it is a labour-intensive task but may just save the day. (Rob Griffin)

The wheels shown controlled speed and direction of travel, known as the wheels of steel. If you look you will see one has two wheels while the other is single – the missing one was somehow removed as a souvenir. (Rob Griffin)

the Senior Rate is a member of the ship's company while the duty male will be from a visiting unit. There also is a twin set-up for the females which is further forward; these have to be provided by visiting units during the silent hours as first point of contact between the cadets and the ship's company.

We at the moment are located on 2 deck and we have only 3 and 4 to visit, so it is up and down ladders and through narrow hatches. 5 deck and area below 5 deck will not be visited due to the constraints of H&S and the fact there is not a lot to see of interest anyway. Arriving back at the laundry area, or *dhobi* in naval parlance, we are greeted by a large hatch, down which we now make our way down and arrive on 3 deck: this is

This is the view that a visitor would have on approaching HMS *Bristol*. To gain access from the main HMS Excellent base you sound a buzzer that alerts HQ1, and they can view you by CCTV. If satisfied they press a button and a gate opens, allowing you to walk along the floating jetty till you reach the aforementioned stairs to HQ1. (Tommy Lee Shiels)

Ship Control Centre from another angle – as can be seen by all the dials and controls, it certainly lives up to its name. (Victoria Jones)

very much the technical side of the ship and around midships we come upon a large area full of screens and dials: we have reached the Ship's Control Centre (SCC), often referred to

After the Falklands refit when all the ship's boats were removed, additional life raft stowage was fitted with these being at the stern end of 1 deck. (HMS *Bristol*)

as the heart of the ship. If the bridge of a ship is considered its eyes, and the operations room its brain, there is no doubt that the SCC is the beating heart. It is from the SCC that all machinery from propulsion to sewage is controlled by a team of marine engineers who are likely to man the compartment 24 hours a day, every day, while at sea.

In a combat scenario the SCC becomes the headquarters, where all the information from across the ship, be it fire, flood or casualty is reported, and priorities are set on where to send repair teams. This all happens during the battle, to maintain 'power to command', allowing the ship to conduct her primary tasking, whatever it may be. Also located here is a small portioned-off compartment which houses the emergency steering position – a further

The signal deck showing one of the signal lamps in its protective cover. Note the wooden grille deck and the bank of speakers and boxes – ideal reference for modellers. (HMS *Bristol*)

Although moored using a fixed system, *Bristol* retains her anchor and all the chains associated with operating them. In this view the starboard chain can be seen coming out of the bonnet and around the capstan. (Rob Griffin)

No luxury spared! This tip-up wash basin in an officer's cabin, with hot and cold taps, could be folded up against the bulkhead to provide a bit more space. (Rob Griffin)

position is located in the steering tiller flat. The space is filled with monitors and dials that allow the state of the ship to be monitored at all times. Leaving the SCC, we move further forward until we come to the operations room, where again there are lots of IT screens for the officers responsible in their part of the ship. The ops room is vital to the ship's defence and safety, enabling *Bristol* to defend herself and others: it could be said that the ops room is the electronic eyes and ears of the ship, it is from here that the captain will fight his ship, rather than the traditional image of from the bridge.

We now make our way back to where we alighted onto 3 deck and take the plunge down another set of ladders till we reach 4 deck. In front of us is a sign telling us that

beyond this door is the Sea Dart theatre. Most will not know what to expect, and the sight that greets them is amazing, for this is an amazing conservation of the past and present. The original deck of the Sea Dart magazine cannot be seen as it is covered by a cinema-style sloping floor, where located either side are comfortable cinema-style seats. The very bottom is level and on that area is located a podium and controls for a large screen which unrolls from the deck head. Beyond this on either side are the original feeds for the missiles, which would be moved to these hoists by the magazine feed that held the missiles; the type would be selected by the control officer whose window onto the magazine can just be seen on the top right behind a large poster. Once

A first-class shot showing the view from the helmsman's position on the bridge; it also shows the size of the fibreglass moulding over the Sea Dart tracker. (Rob Griffin)

the missiles selected were in place and positioned on the hoist, the blast doors on the launcher would open and the missiles would be raised onto the launcher arm; it would return ready for the next two and the blast doors would close and the procedure would start over again; this happened very quickly and so as to minimise time, the flash doors were open to the outside. This theatre is used for all sorts of briefings and training and is a wonderful facility.

Leaving the Sea Dart theatre, we move forward again, and pass such stores that are no longer used for their original purpose but must conjure up memories, such as the beer store: nothing more needs to be said on that.

4 and 5 decks are the main machinery spaces, and it is here that the gas turbines,

gearboxes, steam turbines and boiler rooms are located. Although changes have been made to accommodate the cadets, such as segregation of the sexes, one nice touch is in most places the retention of the old mess numbers; for example, on 3 deck forward are 3 and 4 messes, 3E and 3DZ, now female accommodation, which might raise eyebrows for the those who used to live there.

We then pass the access to the gas turbine spaces, gearing spaces and steam turbine spaces; access to these areas for cadets is normally restricted unless escorted by a member of the ship's company. We are allowed a look inside and for those who have never seen inside the engineering spaces of a warship the first comment is usually, 'Wow!' This is because every inch is taken up with machinery, pipes, and valves. Looking in the gas turbine spaces, we can see the mounting frame where one of the Olympus gas turbines was located but sadly the area has been left to slowly fade away as it's no longer in use. While we explore these levels, we are also shown the empty space and hydraulic rams that once controlled the stabilisers – again they and propellors were removed when *Bristol* became a training ship. Looking into the gear spaces, the first thing we notice is the size of the gearboxes – up till then we probably have thought in terms of car gearboxes, but these are massive, and a reminder of how something as simple as a small foreign object could damage them. A contraband box is at the entrance, in which cigarettes, lighters and any items not needed while working on the boxes were placed. On completion of a task. all tools had to be accounted for.

If we were to continue forward, we would come to the 4.5-gun area but again sadly little remains of this and the actual shaft of the gun is now a 'place to hide things' and the magazines are out of bounds to virtually all.

We turn around and head to the very stern of the ship to the steering gear compartment; again, the sheer size and strength of the components is mind-boggling. The arms are painted green and red for starboard and port. Also located here is the final emergency steering location – one is on the bridge, one in the SCC and this one, so plenty of back-up. The remaining decks are crew-only access, so we make our way back topside and the fresh air.

I think most are amazed that when you look at *Bristol* as from outside, she appears huge, but this short walk around has definitely changed that outlook. Although the spaces are as she is now, not too much cutting and removing has taken place, so most areas are recognisable to the old and bold, and many images show ex-crew happily in their old mess and in some cases their old bunk.

CHAPTER 4

THE SOUTH ATLANTIC

HMS *Bristol* off South Georgia, carrying out a VERTREP (vertical replenishment) with a Chinook heavy-lift helicopter. During the deployment south much cross-loading of stores had to take place to ensure that the correct stores were in the correct ship. (HMS *Bristol*)

HMS *Bristol* moving up alongside for a fuel RAS (Replenishment at Sea), which could comprise fuel or solid stores such as ammunition, food and spare equipment. This system allows the ships to remain at sea for far longer and cover greater distances. (HMS *Bristol*)

During 1981 HMS *Bristol* participated in Exercises *Spring Train* and *Ocean Safari* which took in some excellent runs ashore, including Mayport, Fort Lauderdale, Norfolk, Lisbon, Porto, Amsterdam, Hull, and Portland

As well as participating in the exercises and visits to these fantastic ports, she was still also carrying out missile firings; however, in November of that year she went into the dockyard for a 28-week assisted maintenance period, which she was well due: throughout her life many had referred to her as the white elephant of the fleet, and to some extent they had a point – she was a large ship and as the only one of her kind and with no real defined role, she was costly both in terms of the manpower needed to crew her and the cost of maintaining her. So, no sooner had she docked, and the work commenced, than the duty buzz (someone on board always knew what was going to happen and so the duty buzz started; more often than not it was wrong) was that she would complete this period then be laid up with a view to being sold for scrap, which was supposed to be contained in the Defence Review for 1981.

However, a certain General Galtieri inadvertently came to her rescue for in April 1982, the Argentine armed forces invaded the Falkland Islands, safe in the knowledge that their assessment had shown that Britain was losing interest in the islands, with furthw er evidence being the imminent withdrawal of the Royal Navy Ice Patrol vessel HMS *Endurance* – in Argentina's eyes this was proof enough that Britain would not intervene. History showed this ranks as one of the biggest military misunderstandings of all time, for within three days of the invasion the first part of a task force left British waters heading for the South Atlantic: this included two aircraft carriers, the venerable HMS *Hermes* and the new HMS *Invincible*.

At first it was thought this would not involve *Bristol* but that soon changed. HMS *Bristol* was alongside at Portsmouth and at 48 hours' notice to steam, most of the crew were on leave taking

With the snow-capped hills in the background, this view shows how desolate the Falklands and South Georgia can be, but with a beauty of their own. (HMS *Bristol*)

The port-side 20-mm Oerlikon gunner getting some practice, on the way south. At this time the 20 mm was the only secondary armament apart from a jury-rigged GPMG or LMG. A much better fit of secondary armament would be applied to RN ships on their return to the UK as a result of experiences in the Falklands.

The famous Bobo the cormorant that adopted the ship during her time down south. It was named after the mechanical owl in the film *Clash of the Titans*. (HMS *Bristol*)

advantage of the break for the refit, and they like many others from all the services arrived home to either find telegrams waiting for them or a police officer knocking on the door telling them to return to the ship immediately. While the crew knew the most probable reason for the recall, I know some have spoken of the police not being too subtle on picking the destination, and the strange looks that those around gave them. Here are a few comments on the recall from some of *Bristol*'s crew:

Dave Walsh: I was in bed after a night 'on it'. My mum came in and said someone has just phoned and said, 'Can you tell him to get his arse back down to Pompey [navy slang for Portsmouth] asap.' So I did. Not 100 per cent sure why the recall but had a fair idea.

Jim Bellew: I was on Easter leave, got a phone call whilst up a ladder painting mum and dad's window frames. Return to Osprey asap, do leaving routine and join the *Bristol* in Pompey. Colin Prudhoe I remember being on leave, but don't recall being called to come back early … Maybe because I was a baby tiff [slang for artificer] I do remember we were told initially that we would not be going south, and that worked out well, didn't it.

Alan Carpenter: I had a knock on the door Sunday morning with a roast just about to go in, a crusher [service or civilian policeman] was there and told me that I was needed on the ship.

Russ Hall: I was duty weekend prior to the Monday we sailed. Spent it dangling on a paint stage painting the black upper part of the main 992 mast grey! That mast is very tall!

Mark Kempson: I was on board when it was announced we would be off! Thought the Falklands were near the Shetlands!

HMS *Bristol* and HMS *Invincible* getting a bit too close for comfort, although in this case it is the perspective that is at fault and not the seamanship. (John Dodd/ HMS *Bristol*)

The refit was very hastily cut short, and *Bristol* sailed for post-refit trials on 15 April, where a faulty fuel pump was discovered and very quickly rectified. Once the trials were completed, she Stored and made ready to sail. It must have seemed strange to be on the white elephant and sailing to a war zone; although it is something we have at the back of our minds when we join, we never think it will happen to us. Other memories are of the crowds that lined the shore to wave goodbye and wish us good luck and come home soon. But none thought it would actually come to a shooting war.

HMS *Bristol* finally left Portsmouth heading for the Falklands Islands on 10 May 1982. Here are some brief details outlining HMS *Bristol*'s role during the conflict in diary form:

Monday 10th May 1982

HMS Bristol departs Portsmouth with the fleet tanker RFA [Royal Fleet Auxiliary are civilian-crewed ships that support the fleet at sea and can provide almost anything a ship needs, from a can of soft drink to tons of fuels] Olna. The Type 21 Frigates Active & Avenger along with the Leander Class Frigates, Andromeda and Minerva & Penelope who departed from Devonport. The whole group was designated CTU 318.8

Wednesday 12th May 1982

The Type 42 Destroyer Cardiff sails from Gibraltar and joins up with the group on Friday.

Friday 14th May 1982

After a fast passage south the Bristol group arrive at Ascension Island over Tuesday and

The idea is I think is to load it into the launcher tube and not fire from the shoulder. (HMS *Bristol*)

Wednesday the 18th & 19th of May. During the trip South quite a few of the crew had their birthdays, one such memorable birthday was to Patrick Simcoe, who on Ascension Island was very touched that he had been remembered when his mess presented him with an 18th birthday cake, covered in icing and lashings of cream. A knife was handed to him to cut the cake, and as he cut into it, he realised it was nothing more than a well decorated cardboard box! Once the mess had picked themselves up from the deck where they had ended up in fits of laughter, they presented him with a real cake, Patrick says, 'It certainly was a birthday to remember' however the break time was brief and on the 21st May at around 0900 RFA Tidespring hastening forward after getting rid of prisoners from South Georgia [this action had already taken place and the South Georgia islands were once again flying the Union flag] joins the Bristol group.

An Aircraft is detected which is not an Airliner although it was a Boeing 727 being used in the Long-Range Maritime reconnaissance role as its track plot took the form of a series of loops and curlicue's, which brought the Aircraft in from over 200 miles to within 35 miles, its closest point of approach. Captain A. Grose RN leading the group ordered HMS Cardiff to drop back and altered the disposition of the ships to disguise her 'disappearance'. The Aircraft duly obliged by coming within extreme range of the Type 42 which engaged the target at about 1230Z with Sea Dart, although no hit was made the aircraft veered away very sharply, and after the war it was discovered that they had had a very close call.

What every well-dressed sailor is wearing down South Atlantic way. Note the use of anti-flash hood and gloves, overall and thick socks, leaving only the narrow slit for the eyes, protecting as much skin as possible. (HMS *Bristol*)

By Wednesday the 26th May the Bristol group has joined the main Task Force to more than make up for ships that have been lost. All ships are given their tasks, and some take up positions giving N.G.S. [Naval Gun Fire Support, a traditional role for the Royal Navy] in support of troop activities on the Islands.

Friday 28th May 1982

HMS BRISTOL is detached to take up station as 'LOLA Manager' [Logistics Operating Local Area] to defend and manage the R.F.A's and S.T.U.F.T. [this amusing abbreviation is Ships Taken Up From Trade – these were civil vessels such as the liners *Queen Elizabeth* and Canberra, to tankers and all types of ships], ensuring that ships bound for the battle group or A.O.A. [Amphibious Operating Area] were available, had the appropriate instructions and were ready to leave on time.

Saturday 29th May 1982

The County Class Destroyer HMS Glamorgan relieves HMS Bristol as 'LOLA Manager'.

A Royal Fleet Auxiliary vessel making headway in typical South Atlantic weather of the sort that Bristol and all the ships deployed had to endure. (HMS Bristol)

HMS *Bristol* following HMS *Invincible* in the South Atlantic. Note all the forward railings are in the action stations position to ensure clear arcs of fire. (Peter Featherstone Williams)

Thursday 3rd June 1982

The Bristol group takes 32hrs to carry out replenishments, with RFA Plumleaf connected to one or other warship for 22 of those hours.

During her sojourn down south *Bristol* managed to stay unscathed but did achieve a Sea Dart strike on a passing cloud, which might sound very unprofessional but at the time spurious images were constantly appearing, and ever mindful of the fate of HMS *Sheffield*, *Coventry* and the *Atlantic Conveyor*, it was often deemed prudent to launch

After the Argentine surrender, HMS *Bristol* remained on station making two short stops at San Carlos and Port Stanley. On 1 July Admiral Woodward was relieved

as commander of the task force by Rear Admiral Reffell who had transferred to HMS *Bristol* from the *Isis* which had brought him up from Ascension. Rear Admiral Reffell then transferred his flag over to *Illustrious*. *Bristol* then began the long journey home on 28 August. After an overnight stop at Ascension for an SODS (Ship's Operatic Drama Society) opera, HMS *Bristol* along with *Invincible* and *Olna* continued north, arriving back in Portsmouth on 17 September to be met by Her Majesty Queen Elizabeth II. They also received a rousing welcome from those watching all along the sea front and the famous Round Tower, something that will remain with them forever.

As always there is a lighter side to any conflict, and this is one such tale, as remembered by Stephen Beeny:

A shot from happier times – the former Limbo mortar well that was converted into the ship's swimming pool; sadly, once *Bristol* was warned off for South Atlantic duty, this had to go and was plated over to create a strengthened landing spot for helicopters. (HMS *Bristol*)

An unexpected visitor was a Cormorant which crash landed onto the GDP [Gun Director Platform]. My understanding is Geoff Mackett was the OOW that night, he was also the ship's diving officer (of which I was one of, in fact I was diver's yeo) [yeoman], that is how I came to look after her. I say her, as when we started northwards and it started getting warmer the bloody thing started making a nest out of the old gash bags and shreddies from the MCO [Material Control Officer], which I used in the diving store to clean up her projectile shitting. Nice! This was probably not helped by the food given her, which included defrosted (sometimes) rainbow trout, prawns, and any other variety of seafood the wardroom galley could supply. She would sit there panting away and I would try and cool her down by filling the massive sink in the store with sea water where she would sit and bob backwards and forwards depending on the sea state. The chippy built a canvas crossing the line pool on the flight deck, but Bobo was banned after she crapped in it twice. She got her name incidentally not from bobbing about, but from the mechanical owl in *Clash of the Titans* film released the year before, which we took down south with us. There is a scene when it falls off the branch and lays crumpled on the floor, apparently the booties [RN slang for the Royal Marines] and her rescuers on that night thought it up! She would follow me around the upper deck, waddling along behind and the lads were quite taken with her. I was always worried she would do a bobo overboard and that would have been it; we were in quite a hurry to get home, I remember.

On arrival in Pompey, two London zookeepers came on board and took her away and she was put in quarantine. About a month later

HMS *Bristol* alongside *Stena Inspector*. This ship was used as a floating repair base and the concept proved very successful. In 1983, she was bought by the UK government and refitted and entered service as RFA *Diligence*. She served the fleet till she was put up for disposal in June 2016. (Trevor Sharpe/ HMS *Bristol*)

Geoff Mackett and I were invited up to the zoo for a handing-over ceremony. We had the usual interviews with the papers – *Sun*, *Mirror*, *Telegraph*, *Times* etc. but my best gizzit [Jackspeak, or sailor talk, for a freebie] was a Blue Peter badge given me by Simon Groom (that interview was never screened). We also got a good lunch with the zoo's boss and n

Navy PR woman. Bobo was put into a large open pen, with other odds and sods from around the world. She was last seen by us waddling round the pool. The next we heard was in about December when we were informed that she had got an infection and sadly died – a memorable end to a momentous time.

This tale shows how avid souvenir-hunting service personnel can be, even if it is not a good idea at times.

Stuart Bush remembers:

It's a while ago but memorable; we managed to get an hour in Port Stanley after the surrender, the ship was anchored in Stanley Bay and a few chefs and others caught the boat in for a look-around to see what all the fuss had been about and see if the lesser services had left anything worth lifting. Anyway, at the end of our allotted time we drifted back towards the jetty with little bits and pieces when John Parks comes up with a bloody great roll of stinking cam netting over his shoulder, wouldn't tell anyone what was in it but wanted to sit in the middle of the crowd so when we got back to the ship, he would be less conspicuous. Well, it took a bit of physical and light-hearted persuasion to get the netting off while on the pas boat to reveal the arse end of all four feet of a

HMS *Bristol* firing her Sea Dart missile. Although not a Falklands shot, it shows the effect of firing. She fired two missiles in anger on 22 May 1983 although it seems it was a spurious contact. (HMS *Bristol*)

Evidence that combat is not as clean as video games portray: the badly burned and damage RFA *Sir Tristram*, which along with RFA *Sir Galahad* suffered the attack in Bluff Cove when many were killed on both ships. She was returned to the UK by heavy lift ship, was extensively refitted and then returned to service. In December 2005, she was decommissioned but now is permanently moored in Portland harbour and is used for training Special Forces. (HMS *Bristol*)

The welcome home for all the task force ships was highly emotional and no ship came in alone: each was escorted by a flotilla of boats containing well-wishers as can be seen by this view of HMS *Bristol*. (HMS *Bristol*)

Rapier missile – what a magnificent souvenir! So John gets it up the starboard waist ladder and down the mess via the flight deck and past the FD [Flight Deck] crew, so he didn't go unnoticed. So down 3RFWD mess the chefs are working out where to hang this thing when the Tannoy goes off: 'Cook Park report to the STBD [starboard] waist and bring your souvenir with you.' Up goes John full of the joys with his new toy to be met by numerous people including the weapons officer who upon seeing said item started shouting at him to heave the thing over the rail. It's still there somewhere to this day, but John didn't

get into any bother – just a few choice words I believe, because we were all told before going ashore not to touch anything because of booby traps, but hell! if it ain't nailed down. On the way home in the north side of the Bay of Biscay early evening there was a pipe that the quarterdeck for an hour was to be available to anyone who needed to get rid of anything they had picked up on the islands that they shouldn't have, because when we got home no leave would be granted until customs had gone through the ship like a dose of salts and woe betide anyone caught … and the only customs we saw was some

HMS *Bristol* follows HMS *Invincible* into Portsmouth Dockyard, surrounded by hundreds of well-wishers in craft of all shapes and sizes, which must have created headaches for the MoD Police. The actual docking would have been challenging for the crews as well. (HMS *Bristol*)

Public enthusiasm welcoming the task force ships home safe and sound. (Russ Hall)

bod waving on the Round Tower, grrrr. Last one we also got ashore for an hour on San Carlos water, so I was having a bloody cold bimble around when this damm Rapier battery started following me; thought it was just doing its thing, so I moved the other way and round it came again. You get a bit worried, don't you? So, after a few minutes of this I hears laughter and found a couple of squaddies in a trench with the thing on manual … put the bloody willies up me.

Possibly the last word goes to Mike Tuttiett from the Association:

I think the deployment down south made quite a few boys into men, and already men into stronger men. Some will have good and bad memories, and some haunting ones which I hope will not trouble them too greatly. But we will never forget those who will not return. A 'Band of Brothers' never to be broken whatever service they were in.

Commissions

HMS *Bristol* docked at Leningrad during a 1989 deployment; judging from the tales it seems the Russians could not get enough of her. (HMS *Bristol*)

I decided that where possible I would let those who were actually there tell their tales; however, many of the bits could not be printed due to the salty nature: some tales are best left in the wardroom/mess.

Avonmouth and Fishguard:

Jeff Fox: I was on board November '74 and used to go home weekenders to South Wales, joyously telling my family that I had been drafted to HMS *Bristol* when I got in at about 8 pm, to which the reply was, 'Ooh, is that the HMS *Bristol* that's on fire at Milford Haven?' After the fire we just did Fishguard, Guzz [Devonport], a trip to Rotterdam, Liverpool and Avonmouth. While at Avonmouth, ship open to visitors one

afternoon, loads of panic on the gangway as one of the gangway staff, can't remember whether it was the OOD [Officer Of the Deck], recognised someone in the queue, it was Lord Louis Mountbatten, hustled him on board and straight into the warrant officers' mess where I had the honour as duty mess man to serve him a cup of coffee. Also, while on board there was a ship's group, 'Air Stream' I think, we played Whale Island bops and had a full programme in the Liverpool club ship *Landfall* in the docks every night.

Stephen Beeny: This tale of some inept sailors, is getting somewhat faded now. But here we go. I remember sometime in 1974 being part of an 'exped' during Sea Dart trials at Fishguard.

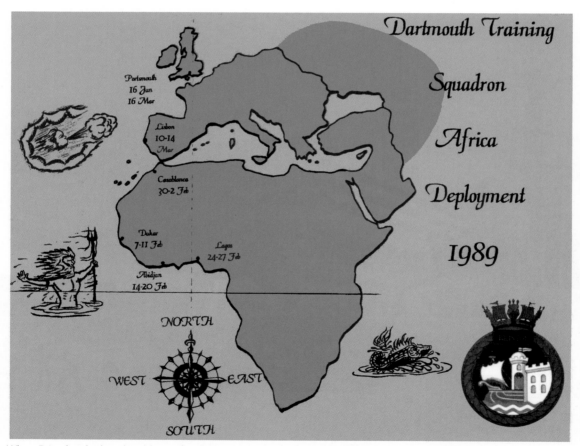

When *Bristol* and other ships depart for deployments, maps are often created showing the deployment and places that will be visited. These are sometimes used in commission books to show loved ones what has been going on. This one is from her days as the Dartmouth Training Squadron Deployment, 1989. (HMS *Bristol*)

When HMS *Bristol* visited her namesake city, the nearest she could get was to Avonmouth and for that she docked using a stern approach due to the limited area for manoeuvre. (HMS *Bristol*)

I was a 17-year-old A/B [Able Seaman] radar and volunteered to crew one of those three-ton workboats on 'exped' while the *Bristol* went off into Cardigan Bay playing with the Sea Dart system. We were on the davit very early one morning, weather not particularly good, packing the workboat with packed lunches and tinnies. I don't recall any names for this 'jolly', but my PO [Petty Officer] part of ship was in charge (a PO RP) [Petty Officer Regulating Police] and there were possibly about eight to a dozen of on this, seaman, chefs, stokers etc. We expected to land somewhere and have a jolly old time exploring the local beauty spots. So, the boat was dropped off the davit and we toddled away and followed the coastline south-west looking for a suitable place to land. We tried to land on a beach somewhere a few miles down the coast, but the breakers were dumping too heavy on the shoreline, so we gave that up and tried for somewhere else. We eventually came to an inlet to a secluded bay which looked rather nice, and I recall there may have been a building on the hillside which we thought might have been a pub! We sailed on into the bay and anchored there in high tide and went ashore (not sure how we got from the workboat to shore but I think

we may have a small inflatable or something). Anyway, we went off walking and exploring around the area, no pub, and came back some time later. To our surprise, the tide and gone out and the workboat was high and dry, banked on its side on the sandy, rocky bay … oops! Well, we just have to wait for the tide to come back in and we'll be back off to join *Bristol* later in Fishguard Bay a few miles up the coast … easy! We walked across the now-dry bay to inspect the workboat. Oh dear! the individual propellers had come off the workboat shaft and were now lying across the sand and rocks. They obviously had been knocked off as the workboat settled down on the rocks as the tide fell … Oh shit! Luckily, we had a stoker with us, and he went on to attempt to fix the props back on to the shaft – job done easy, back up to Fishguard to join the *Bristol*, nobody the wiser. We set off when the tide had given us sufficient water in the bay to get us on our way back up the coastline. The workboat, however, was not 'playing ball', sluggish and slow, but we eventually got out of the bay, but sea conditions were a little heavy and the workboat was still not playing ball; we were unable to make headway and realised we were being pushed toward the rocks. Oh shit! In the panic someone decided to call May Day on the radio. We did however manage to closely avoid the rocks and after some time get back to the shelter of the bay, where we were greeted with a Coast Guard Land Rover driving down the rough track to greet us. Sometime after we had anchored in the bay, we saw the *Bristol* appear just off the bay in response to our May Day call – postponed the trials to come look for us; this did not bode well for the man in charge! After we were taken back on board, I recall that the engineers found that the blades on the workboat prop had not been put back on at the right pitch, hence the sluggishness and inability to make headway.

Antwerp:

Bill Dickson: In Amsterdam ('73), a group of admirals, generals etc. came on board and Commander E. Robertson conducted them to the PO stokers' (2GStbd) mess to drink beer and have the crack. At about noon, a message came down from the wardroom to say that

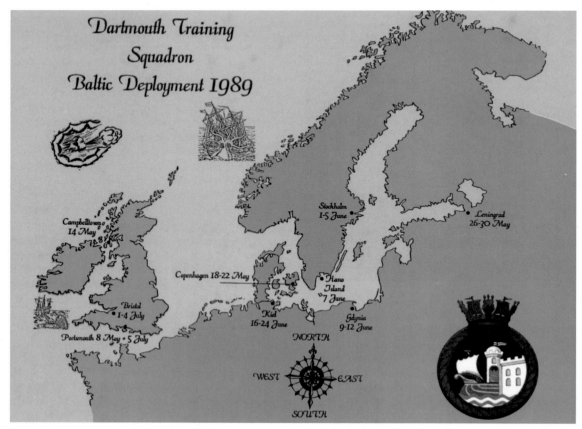

The deployment map for the Dartmouth Training Squadron in 1989. These maps show that joining the navy still offers the allure of travel. (HMS *Bristol*)

HMS *Bristol* approaching Port Said. (HMS *Bristol*)

In tropical climes.

One of the perils during an RN deployment is that if you are crossing the line (equator) for the first time, then you will get a visit from King Neptune and his court. Lots of fun and antics with no one spared – even the Princesses Elizabeth and Margret were caught up in it on HMS *Vanguard*, albeit to a lesser degree. Victims have their 'crimes' read out, lathered up by the barber then into the pool for a good soaking. (HMS *Bristol*)

During many of these visits the ship is usually open for some of the time which usually brings the crowds en masse. This shows just such a scene and although taken on Navy Day, it is representative of the crowds that can be expected. (Rob Griffin)

lunch was ready. About 30 minutes later, the skipper dispatched an officer to prise them out – presumably, they were enjoying the beer!

Gibraltar:

Alan Eyres: I was on board then as a killick greenie [a killick is slang for a sailor rated as a Leading Hand – he wears a fouled anchor as rank badge; a greenie is an electrical trained person from the Marine Engineering Branch]. The whites were for ceremonial divisions. Captain's inspection of the whole ship's company whilst alongside in Gib. I got ready and went to fall in on the flight deck and the

guy next to me collapsed. Told by the Chief Greenie [Chief Petty Officer electrician] to take him below and stay with him, so that was a waste of time ironing the ice-cream suit in the first place, but there is a large b/w photo of the ship and ship's company taken straight afterwards.

Madeira:

Steve Greenley: Went to Madeira on *Bristol* in 1973; it was her first real foreign trip if you discount Antwerp.

Craig Quilliam: I just made it back on board five minutes before sailing –after Trev told the OOD the hotel name where I ended up. And the note on the hotel bar table read, 'A day without wine is a day without sunshine – why not a carafe of wine?'

Isle of Man / Bristol / Milford Haven / 1975-6 Portsmouth refit / 1977 refit / Rededication, Tuesday, 4 November:

Jeff Fox: Forward greenies' mess 1977 while watching Sid James in *Bless this House*; someone in mess commented on a nice young lady in the programme, Linda Cunningham, and suggested we write to her and invite her to be mess pinup. She replied and only said yes.

Dunkirk, / Liverpool / Bermuda / Nassau / Freeport / West Palm Beach / Mayport / Norfolk / St John's / Portsmouth:

Paul Mann: I remember getting married in August 1978 and going on deployment to USA on 30 August. We went to Norfolk and a few other places such as Norfolk, Charleston, and Wilmington

Paul Finch: That was the year [1978] we also went to West Palm Beach, Nassau, Freeport and very short stop-off in Halifax on the way back. I remember we took a road trip from Norfolk to Okracoke, North Carolina, to take some ensigns to a British naval grave.

Hamburg:

Ian Robinson: We were in Hamburg in early 1979. My first run ashore in the mob and onboard the *Bristol*. First stop, window shopping down the Reeperbahn and an eye opener that was – great times though.

Exercise Spring Train: Mayport / Charleston / Wilmington / Norfolk / Bristol:

Willie Wonka: We played rugby against Cape Fear in a stadium; after the game, challenged Yanks to drinking game known as BOAT RACE,

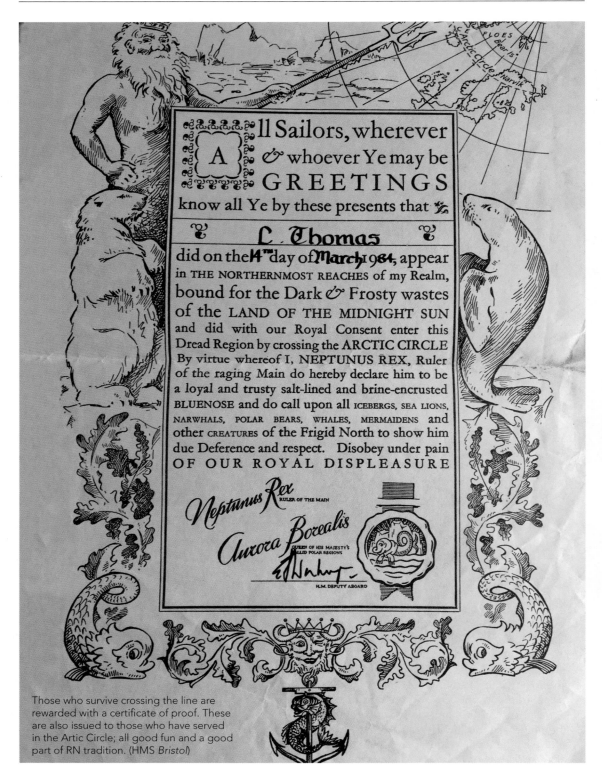

All Sailors, wherever & whoever Ye may be GREETINGS know all Ye by these presents that

L. Thomas

did on the 14th day of March 1984, appear in THE NORTHERNMOST REACHES of my Realm, bound for the Dark & Frosty wastes of the LAND OF THE MIDNIGHT SUN and did with our Royal Consent enter this Dread Region by crossing the ARCTIC CIRCLE By virtue whereof I, NEPTUNUS REX, Ruler of the raging Main do hereby declare him to be a loyal and trusty salt-lined and brine-encrusted BLUENOSE and do call upon all ICEBERGS, SEA LIONS, NARWHALS, POLAR BEARS, WHALES, MERMAIDENS and other CREATURES of the Frigid North to show him due Deference and respect. Disobey under pain OF OUR ROYAL DISPLEASURE

Neptunus Rex
RULER OF THE MAIN

Aurora Borealis
QUEEN OF HIS MAJESTY'S ALLIED POLAR REGIONS

H.M. DEPUTY ABOARD

Those who survive crossing the line are rewarded with a certificate of proof. These are also issued to those who have served in the Artic Circle; all good fun and a good part of RN tradition. (HMS *Bristol*)

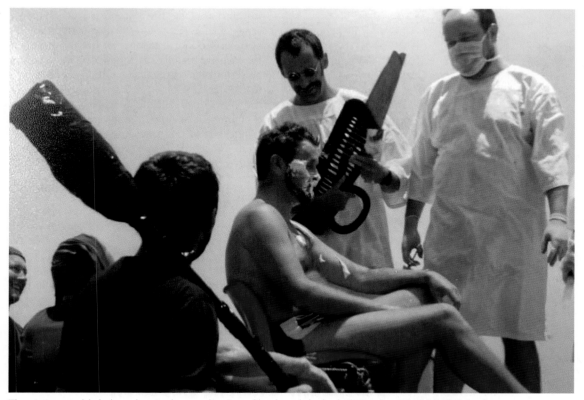

The victim suitably lathered up is about to be tipped back and dunked. H&S, what H&S? (HMS *Bristol*)

six on each team with a pitcher of beer for each person, first six to have empty pitchers upside down on their head declared winners. Yanks did it properly, us Brits just tipped pitchers of ale over our heads, declared ourselves the winners. The Yanks' faces were a picture. Also, while at Mayport in 1979, inter-department tug of war competition took place and the winning team were the Comms [Communicators] mess, and this was celebrated with a 'few' cans of beer. Competitions like this were normally held and often included taking on local teams, with varying amount of success.

1980 Refit / COST (Commander Fleet Operational Sea Training) Portland / Liverpool / Mayport / Charleston / Wilmington / Norfolk / Bristol / Wilhelmshaven / Hull / Exercise Ocean Safari (1981):

Patrick Simcoe: I joined Bristol at 17 years old in 1981, my first ship out of training from HMS *Mercury*. We sailed for America within a

few weeks of my joining. On the first night at sea, the pipe came from the bridge to darken ship; the leading hand of the mess said, 'Go and turn the lights off, Pat, we have to darken ship.' I started going round turning off each light individually, no he said, 'No, turn them off at the main switches.' So off I trotted like a good little sailor, and turned off all the lights on the main switches to 4R port, centre and starboard. 4R was an S&S mess, and they were shouting, 'What the bloody hell's happened to the lights?' I had darkened ship when we were three decks below the waterline – that was my first bite.

Mayport / Fort Lauderdale / Norfolk / Lisbon / Porto / Amsterdam / Hull / Portland / Annual Maintenance Period / Portland BOST (Basic Operational Sea Training)/ Falklands Conflict / Freedom of Bristol / Greenwich / Bremerhaven / Exercise Carribtrain (1983) / Wilmington / Grand Cayman / Trinidad and

This picture needs no caption but is typical of the departmental groups during a deployment or commission. (HMS *Bristol*)

Tobago / Guadalupe / Grand Turk / Puerto Rico / Gibraltar:

Roy Lane: First thing that springs to mind out sightseeing on Gibraltar, a rock ape grabbed my camera and a tug of war ensued. Not wanting to lose the camera, I did the only thing a matelot could do and punched the ape square in the face; it let go and recoiled backwards, falling off the wall it was sat on and tumbling down the rather steep slope to the ledge below. It then stumbled across the ledge like a drunken sailor and fell off that and out of sight. It loses something in the telling but at the time, it was hilarious, it was so funny see this ape stumbling around like a drunken matelot.

Ascension Island / Falklands / Grytviken / Leith / Madeira / Bristol:

Anonymous: Just doing your job can be somewhat hazardous on board, especially when you are young: We sailed for the Falklands in 1982. Whilst loading the ship with stores ready for our voyage, I was in a chain of men, I asked the bloke next to me what happened to all the stores that we were passing up the line; he said they get put on the

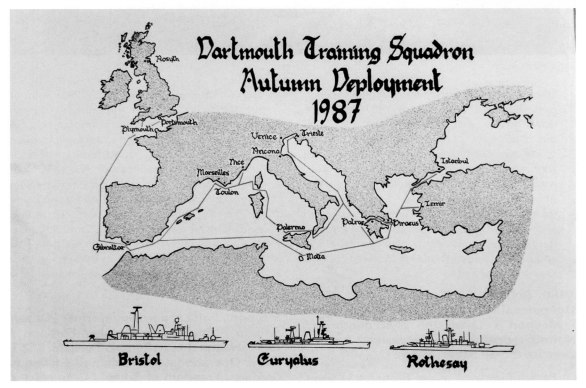

The Dartmouth Squadron autumn cruise looks more like a holiday brochure. It might look glamourous, but a lot of hard work has been put in in between visits. (HMS *Bristol*)

The wonders that can be seen on each deployment are always eagerly anticipated and here is no exception as witnessed by those watching the ship's progress through the Panama Canal. Notice that all are in their tropical white uniforms. (Lance Bower)

lift just over there and they go down five decks to the storage rooms. I walked up to the left and leant over to have a look to see if I could see down, and the next thing I knew one of the guys has hit the emergency stop button – the forks for the lift would be just below my neck as I was looking over and I hadn't realised what was going on, so I came within inches of death and I'm only here due to his quick reactions.

Anonymous: Whilst crashing around the sea in a rigid Sea Rider looks fun, things do not always work out as they should as this tale about being on the rigid Rider down south in 1983 shows. We were going ashore for some IS [Internal Security] training, when the Sea Rider hit a big goffa [wave] which split the rubber section at the front, If I remember right, we were going a little too fast and it was just a touch choppy, and when we landed the inflated section separated from the rigid bottom. We lost some weapons and ammo! Remember singing 'Abide with Me'! Help took ages to come over to us after firing Schermuly flare, and the thing sinking.

We ended up spending a while in the water off San Carlos until a Wessex helicopter picked us up. We were dropped off on an RFA before sea boat transfer back to *Bristol*. And the inevitable mickey taking.

Anonymous: I joined the Royal Navy at 16, only 10 days after leaving school. I chose to be a stoker as my dad had been beforehand. I joined HMS *Bristol* in January 1984, just turned 17, and within days it was due to set sail for America and Canada. I could not believe my luck. My first memory was walking up the gangway and was blown away by the sheer size of her. I remember being shown to the Stokers' Mess and looking around and thinking: how do 70 guys all sleep in here? I was directed to my bunk, a middle bunk; above was a thickset Irish lad (strangely enough called Paddy!) and below was a lad from Newcastle called Geordie (funny that). There was a really old stoker in the mess, who had a long black beard and the lads called him 'Portsmouth' or 'Pompey'. I remember that he had been in

Those on board are getting a grandstand view of the fireworks during *Bristol*'s visit to the USA. (Laurie White)

HMS *Bristol* moored during the New Orleans Expo in 1984. (Laurie White)

the navy for absolutely years, was a legend on board, and had been around the world several times. I also seem to recall that when we got alongside abroad, he didn't really bother to go ashore as he had seen it all previously. When it came to my first watch, I was nervous and justifiably so. As a junior stoker, I was met by the PO who opened a door, and we entered the boiler room; we climbed down several steps of ladders, until we reached the bottom of the two large boilers. The PO passed me a piece of foam, told me to sit on the deck plate, and watch through a glass inspection hatch, as the burners were put into and lit. My job, whilst this process was ongoing, was to watch the process and report a 'flame out'. He explained to me the consequence of a flame out, and what could happen. He then left me. It was dark, cold, and you could hear every groan of the ship. The burners went in with a thud, and I remember looking up at the ladders thinking how fast I could get up them if the 'wheels came off'.

Anonymous: I recall the trip to America and Canada with great fondness, I was 17, and really had my eyes opened. We often went out in tropical uniform. I remember walking into a bar in Houston, and went to the bar to order some beers, and the barman had said that these were on the house. He explained that a group of businessmen sat close by had signalled that they were going to pick up the tab for the whole group of us. I remember being in Nassau and driving through a village where there was clearly real poverty with dead animals on the street, and reaching Paradise Island, which was … paradise. I remember going up the Mississippi and visiting Bourbon Street. The highlight of the Canadian trip was Toronto with all of the ex-pats, and such a friendly welcome. I loved the *Bristol*: she was a great ship, I was made to feel so welcome, and the lads were brilliant. I grew up a lot in those early days. I was always too scared to play Ukkers [a robust navy version of Ludo, but played much more competitively], as I had seen

HMS *Bristol* is not opening fire on the USA although it looks like it by the smoke on her port side. She is firing a salute as she enters harbour, normally done as a mark of respect. (Laurie White)

the fierce row about 'Ludo players' Derogatory nickname for Uckers players who play Ludo rather than Uckers Rules]! The camaraderie was brilliant, and we all stuck together. I left to join HMS *Manchester* in 1985 but jumped at the chance to join *Bristol* again in 1986.

Joint Maritime Course 87 / Norway / Greenwich / Bristol / Azores / Houston / Grand Turk / New Orleans / Mayport / Roosevelt Roads / Wilmington / St Lawrence Seaway / Toronto / Montreal / Quebec, Halifax / Plymouth (boiler explosion again) / Summer ball / 1985 refit / 1986 refit completed March, rededicated Sunday, 12 April / Gibraltar / Marseilles / Genoa / Palermo / Venice / Brest / 1987 Joint Maritime Course / Port of Spain / Barbados / Roosevelt Roads / Virgin Gorda:

Terry McCormack: So, the good ship *Bristol* is anchored off Virgin Gorda and we have been given four hours' daytime leave. Seeing

as I am about to pick up my POWEM's [Petty Officer Weapons Engineering Mechanic] rate, I was considered by some to be an upstanding and responsible Leading Hand (if only they knew). It was with this recommendation that I was therefore detailed off to take a well-known miscreant and good buddy of mine, Chris 'Nobby' Hall, ashore with me. Nobby had been in the rattle [disciplinary confinement] on a regular basis since we had sailed from UK for various infractions and the 'management' had finally relented and allowed him a run ashore in the company of a, wait for it … 'responsible rating' … me. I met him on the gangway, and he was a sight to behold. He sported a shaven head, an oversized Hawaiian shirt and shorts down past his shins, red glasses, a lime green sock and a pink sock and red plastic sandals. The Master at Arms MUST have known this was not going to turn out well. But we were granted leave.

So, ashore we went – a beautiful island for a run ashore where most of the action took place in the marina bar area of Virgin Gorda.

Deployments are not all work and no play: look at this scene of a ship's group rehearsing in perfect weather and catching the sun as well. Notice the two Land Rovers, one each side of the ship. (Matthew Fairweather)

We visited a couple of bars and partook of a few wets, which also included demolishing a bottle of Southern Comfort between us. This was augmented by an American couple who lashed us up to a few rums, just because we were British sailors. Anyway, time passed, and it was just about time to get the liberty boats back to the ship. Both Nobby and I were, as you can imagine, as wobbly as Chinese wardrobes and were enjoying ourselves immensely and entertaining both liberty men and tourists alike with our clown-like antics and foul language, wrestling with each other until we fell off the jetty into the oggin [the sea]. The only route back onto the jetty was by climbing onto a 14ft dory, then onto a yacht, then onto the jetty. Well … that didn't quite happen. Some fool had left the keys in the dory and as we gave each other knowing grins, Nobby took up his position as my crewman and I started the engine and we cast off. To the cheers of the equally drunk liberty men, and the shouts of the boat owner returning form the shops,

'That's my f***ing boat!', we upped revs and headed out of the harbour and set course for the *Bristol*. What followed has gone down in naval history or at the very least in conversation with ex-Bristolians who were on the ship's books at that time.

The first the ship heard of the incident was when the naval patrol radioed the ship to report that LWEM [Leading Weapon Engineer Mechanic] McCormack and WEM [Weapons Engineer Mechanic] Nobby Hall are coming back to the ship in their own transport.' Perhaps it wasn't a terribly good idea to circle the ship as the skipper was taking Flag Officer 1st Flotilla around the old girl at the time but the reception from the boys on board was well worth it. Resounding cheers were heard from the packed guardrails as we circled the ship at high speed, especially when Nobby was heard shouting, 'Round again Cox'n!' After we had narrowly missed the ship's divers, we decided that we had better take 'our' boat away from the immediate area as they had launched two

HMS *Bristol* alongside during her visit to Naples. (Stephen Haddesey)

During deployments and especially on the return trip there is always time for a SODS opera (Ship's Operatic and Drama Society), although nothing could be further from the truth. A show is made up of skits and no one or rank is safe. The makeup and costumes are amazing as are the skits. (Paul de Jonghe)

PITTSBURGH
NEW YORK
WASHINGTON
RICHMOND
NORFOLK
wilmington
CHARLESTON
JACKSONVILLE
TAMPA
MIAMI
KEY WEST
NASSAU

WESTWARD BOUND

BRISTOL

Another variation on the deployment maps, this time actually picturing the ship. (Paul Hill)

Sea Riders to apprehend us. They never actually gave chase. I think that was something to do with the fact that we had bounced over the nearby reef. The next half hour, hour, half a day? (all a blur) was spent enjoying the boating pleasures that the Caribbean is so famous for. I decided to drive the boat at high speed between the hulls of a giant catamaran but had second thoughts when my crewman, Nobby, standing upright and hanging onto the bowline, looked like he was just about to be decapitated. I executed a violent course change to port which resulted in Nobby swan-diving over the side to starboard and losing his beloved red glasses. After my 'man overboard' was rescued, and amid much merriment and giggling, Nobby took charge and had a go at steering, and it was then my turn to face plant into the warm waters of the Caribbean at about 20 knots.

OK, we had had a great laugh, but it was time to go in and face the music. It was only right that I should take the helm and, as we sheepishly nosed our way into the beach, one final gesture was about to unfold. Another shipmate of mine had just picked up his PO and was leading the naval patrol involved in our 'capture'. As we slowly drifted in, Nobby handed him the bowline and they thought it was all over. WRONG, I reversed engines and we went violently astern, and the PO of the patrol went knee deep and almost face first into the water! Bargain! Finally, we gave up. I had to bail out the boat, pay the owner (who thought it was highly amusing, by the way) some money for

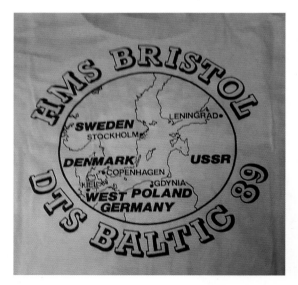

Deployments are always a good occasion to have another T-shirt made to add to the collection (Paul Roebuck)

his damaged prop and await my fate on board, at the next Commander's table. I thought, 'I wonder what the scran [food] is like at DQs [Detention Quarters]?' The look on the Master at Arms face was a picture when he heard what we had done as we were escorted back onto the ship by a rather fuming First Lieutenant.

So, it was the day of the Commander's table and 'Boss Hogg' looked at me and called me a 'f***king toad' and told me not to expect to be rated up to PO anytime soon and I was ANYTHING but a responsible Leading Hand. He also said that we had spoiled his day and the ship's company's day, which was abjectly wrong. HIS day may have been pretty crap, especially when one of our ship's drunken petty officers hurled himself over the side during that evening's Sod's Opera, but our street cred with the ship's company went through the roof! They loved us! Anyway, he lashed me up to 14 days' stoppage [of pay] and

One imagines that life on board a warship is a constant hive of activity with little free time. As this shows this is not always the case and really depends on the tactical situation. During a cruise time is always found for deck games and barbecues. (Peter Williams)

HMS *Bristol* moored at one of her calls in the USA, always a popular deployment location. (HMS *Bristol*)

HMS *Bristol* edging her way through yet another narrow seaway, this time the St Lawrence Seaway. Here, she has just entered one of the seven locks on the St Lawrence. (Chris Prior)

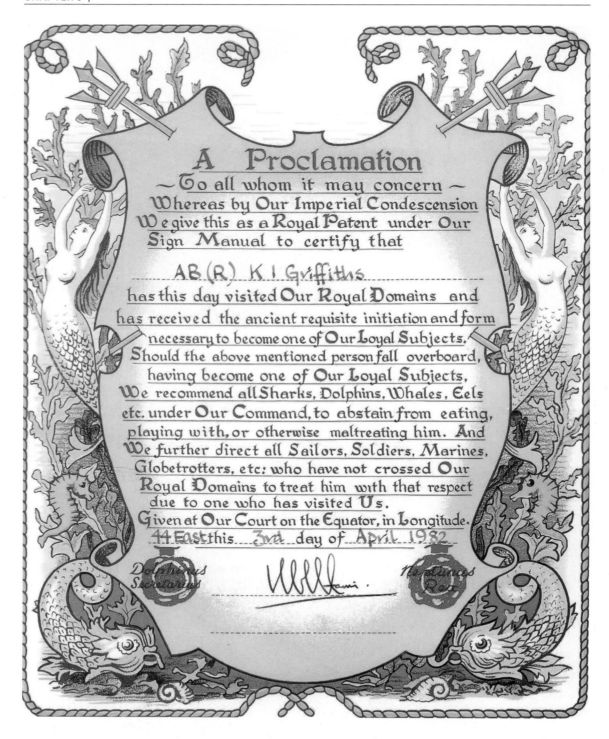

A Proclamation

~ To all whom it may concern ~
Whereas by Our Imperial Condescension
We give this as a Royal Patent under Our
Sign Manual to certify that

AB (R) K I Griffiths

has this day visited Our Royal Domains and
has received the ancient requisite initiation and form
necessary to become one of Our Loyal Subjects.
Should the above mentioned person fall overboard,
having become one of Our Loyal Subjects,
We recommend all Sharks, Dolphins, Whales, Eels
etc. under Our Command, to abstain from eating,
playing with, or otherwise maltreating him. And
We further direct all Sailors, Soldiers, Marines,
Globetrotters, etc: who have not crossed Our
Royal Domains to treat him with that respect
due to one who has visited Us.
Given at Our Court on the Equator, in Longitude.
44 East this 3rd day of April 1982

Davy Jones
Secretarius

Neptunus
Rex

Typical of the type of ship-produced certificate that crew members would receive to show they had crossed the line, although it was not guaranteed to save them next time. (Wikimedia Commons)

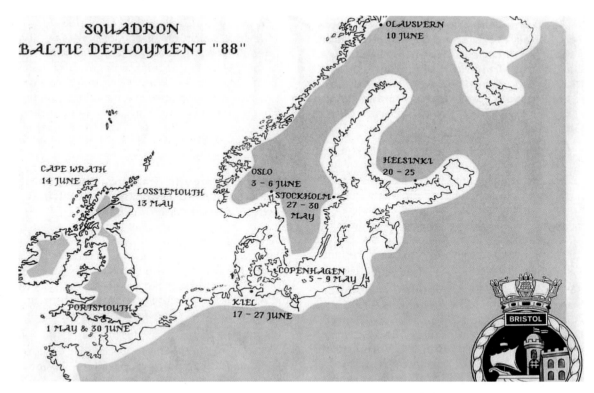

a *50£* fine but the threat to not rate me up to PO never came about. Nobby received 10 days' stoppage. I could have kissed the fat old bastard when he dished out our puns [punishments] AND I was rated up to PO shortly after. We got off very, very lightly but the dit [nickname for a tale or yarn] value that it provided STILL gives me and Nobby fits of giggles 30 years on! Now THAT was a run ashore! ROUND AGAIN COX'N!

Mayport / Wilmington / Converted to Dartmouth training ship for Royal Naval College:

Adam 'Ski' Whitehead: One of the roles of the Dartmouth training ship was to train young officers in their sea duties after they had completed their initial RN training at Dartmouth. On this occasion the young officer was learning the role of Officer Of the Watch, in the early hours, while supervised by training staff with also ship's company doing their normal jobs on the bridge.

The training officer, probably to break the silence, asked: 'Officer Of the Watch, what time is it?'

The reply came back: 'Half past two, sir.'

From the training officer: 'Half past two! That's not very nautical, is it?'

A pause, then the reply: 'Okay, half past two, me hearty.'

At this point staff had to leave the bridge as the struggle to suppress laughter became too much; one wonders how that young officer's career progressed after that.

1987: Britannia Naval College deployment January-April and took in: Port of Spain / Barbados / Roosevelt Roads, Virgin Garda, Mayport Wilmington. This was in company with HMS Euryalus and HMS Rothesay

1988: Dartmouth Training Ship: Caribbean trip 18 January-18 March: Azores / Barbados / Tortilla / San Juan / Castille Islands / Nassau / Wilmington / Bermuda / Azores / Portsmouth; Dartmouth Training Ship: Baltic trip 1 May-30 June: Copenhagen / Lossiemouth / Helsinki / Stockholm / Oslo / Kiel

1989: Dartmouth Training Ship: Africa trip 16 January–16 March: Casablanca Dakar / Abidjan / Lagos, Lisbon / Portsmouth; Dartmouth Training Ship: Baltic trip 8 May–5 July: Campbeltown / Copenhagen / Leningrad / Stockholm / Hano Island / Gydinia / Kid / Bristol, Portsmouth / Guernsey

Vic Vance: Memories of Leningrad. it was great until we decided to open the ship to visitors. The amount of people walking up the gangway in one instance broke the gangway and we had to wait for another. Also, all the hoses (brass nozzles) were nicked from the upper deck and some below on 2 deck. All the request forms and weekend chits nicked from the rack outside the reg office. Nightmare.

1990: Exercise Endeavour 90 / Gibraltar / Suez Canal / Jeddah / Cochin / Singapore / Surataya / Hong Kong / Inchon / Tokyo / Dutch Harbour / Vancouver / San Francisco / Acapulco / Panama Canal / Wilmington / Bermuda / Azores / Portsmouth; Gibraltar guard ship: Lisbon / Gibraltar / Marseilles / Valencia / Naples / Venice / Isamar / Haifa.

During *Endeavour 90*, *Bristol* was being used as a trial ship with WRNS [Women's Royal Naval Service] on board, as women at sea was not the normal thing then so it is easy to imagine how incidents could happen, one such being recounted here:

Dan Kirwan-Taylor: During *Endeavour 90*, we were a Wrens' [Women's Royal Naval Service. Or WRNS] trial ship as part of the DTS [Dartmouth Training Squadron], and we had some Wren officers on board. On the way up to the bridge one afternoon, I saw the Bish (Padre) getting ready for a dhobi [laundry]. The officers' heads had a sign on the door that said, 'Woman in shower, please do not enter.' Well! As the Bish was getting ready, we did not want to hold him up – God's work to do and all that – so we conveniently nicked the young lady's warning sign and float-tested it in the oggin.

From the bridge hatch we could look down into the wardroom flat where we saw him heading for the heads with a towel wrapped around him and his dhobi bag in his hands, not a care in the world. Next thing we hear is a loud female scream emanating from the heads and then the sight of him genuflecting profusely as he scarpered back to his cabin. Poor jenny [feminine of Jack] officer, caught in the nude by the Bish.

1991: Dartmouth Training Ship: Baltic trip: Kristiansand / Stockholm / Helsinki / Aarbus / Amsterdam / Portsmouth

It is a standing joke in forces' circles that whenever a dance or social is organised, the committee will invite the nurses from the local BMH (British Military Hospital) and as part of the folklore, the nurses never ever turn up; however, there is a first time for everything.

Exile Phil: Stockholm 1991, 2L Fwd [Forward] POs' mess social. The much-vaunted busload of nurses actually turned up, to the amazement of the mess, members and just about everyone else onboard. There were so many that we had to enlist members of The Sump [better known as the Stokers' Mess] to help entertain them (leading to at least one subsequent marriage), and as there was only standing room in the mess itself, we needed to ensure that they all spent at least half of their time on board on guided tours, whether they liked it or not. Luckily, Harvey Burwin and Les Crawford, two WE [Weapon Engineering] officers, shimmied down the escape hatch from the wardroom, donned whitefronts and tended the bar for us. We even managed to squeeze in an impromptu performance from the ship's band before being led by our guests to Café Opera in the city centre, where we met Roxette. Tough night that was.

Decommissioned Friday 14 June 1993. Converted to harbour training and accommodation ship and recommissioned Friday, 7 May 1993.

CHAPTER 6

A NEW LIFE

HMS *Bristol* after taking up her role of harbour
training and accommodation ship. She still
carries her 1022 radar array. Where the Corvus
launchers were the back-blast guard and
controls are still fitted. (HMS *Bristol*)

HMS *Bristol* leaving A&P Tyne Yard at Heburn after a refit to give her 10 more years of life, which it certainly did. Radars were removed and both masts truncated, internals were brought up to date with current H&S regulations; oh! and a new coat of paint. (Wikimedia Commons|)

With *Bristol's* conversion and recommissioning as a harbour training ship, she was to have another 27 years providing service to many. What did it all mean though? During her conversion she lost all her armament with the 4.5-inch turret location being plated over; where the Sea Dart launcher was once located a large superstructure was added which contained the sewage treatment plant. The only remaining physical parts of the Sea Dart system are four rails that were used to support the missiles in their shipping containers while being load onto the launcher to be stowed in the magazine and the remains of the magazine that is not the Sea Dart theatre, but lots of the original items have been incorporated into the theatre so it retains some of its past use.

Other changes internally include male and female cadets' heads and accommodation spaces, classrooms and games rooms. HQ1 became the equivalent of the reception. Although the accommodation of cadet groups was a large part of her new role, other tasks undertaken were the use of the ship for anti-terrorist training, diver support and the use of the machinery spaces for training new marine engineers, including how to move heavy machinery around confined spaces. Probably the only disadvantage in her new role was that the galley was non-functioning, so all those staying on board had the trek to either the wardroom or the main galley – fine in the summer but miserable in winter.

It is fair to say that she certainly gave the country its money's worth in her service. The cadets especially loved staying on board and for many it was the first step in joining the Royal Navy. Her small permanent crew of both RN and civilian staff were always helpful to visitors. She underwent a refit at the A&P Hebburn yard on the Tyne; it was intended that this refit was to give her another 10 years' service. Prime tasks carried out including updating her H&S systems and the removal for safety reason of sections of both masts and the removal of the Type 1022 and Type 992Q radars. She

By Sir John Kerr, Knight Commander
Of the Most Honourable Order of
The Bath, Aide-de-Camp, Admiral
In Her Majesty's Fleet and
Commander in Chief of the Naval
Home Command

H.M.S   BRISTOL

Commissioning Order

In pursuance of directions issued by the Admiralty of the defence council, you are hereby to commission Her Majesty's Ship BRISTOL, as a non-seagoing tender to The Commander-in-Chief, Navel Home Command, and are to do so with effect from the seventh day of May 1993 or a date as soon afterwards as circumstances permit.

After the date of commissioning, you will be accountable to the Commodore Her Majesty's Ship NELSON for the discipline, welfare and administration of your Ship's Company and your civilian staff and for the provision of accommodation and boats for members of the Navel Cadet Forces undergoing training in the Portsmouth Area.

You are immediately to bring to the notice of the Commadore, Her Majesty's Ship NELSON any reason you may have for dissatisfaction with the state of the ship generally, or any part of it, and are to invite attention without delay to any other matters of importance, particularly those relating to the welfare of your Ship's Company and your civilian staff.

Given under my hand this seventh day of May 1993 on board Her Majesty's Ship VICTORY, my flag ship, at Portsmouth in the county of Hampshire.

John Kerr

Admiral
Commander-in –Chief
Naval Home Command

To: Lieutenant Commander B Harper, Royal Navy
        HMS BRISTOL.

Information: Parliamentary Under Secretary of State
                    Flag Officer Portsmouth
                    Commodore, HMS NELSON.

HMS BRISTOL SHIP KNOWLEDGE QUIZ

Cadets must be accompanied by an adult when answering this quiz.

The quiz uses Location Markings to assist you find your way around the ship, this note explains how they work.

All warships are divided into decks and sections. In HMS BRISTOL decks are numbered from 01 upwards to 04 and 1 deck down to 5 deck. Sections divide the ship from Bows to Stern and, in HMS BRISTOL, extend from A to T.
For example, HQ1, at the top of the main gangway, is located on 1 deck in section F. HQ1's location marking is therefore 1F.

To complete this quiz you should start at HQ1. Remember, whenever you move up or down a ladder you should have **three** points of contact (ie. two hands and one foot or two feet and one hand!) and you must face the ladder. **Do Not** go up or down with your back towards the ladder!

1.	Looking forward, what does the door marked 1 D provide entry to?	
2.	Moving to the port side, what are the two types of life saving equipment available to assist somebody who may fall over board?	
3.	Move aft and through the door marked 1 J Port. Answer the following questions - 1. When was HMS BRISTOL launched? 2. How many men served onboard?	
4.	Move forward through the fire door on the Port Side to 1 H. Answer the following questions - 1. Who is the Commanding Officer of HMS BRISTOL? 2. When was the first and most recent battle honour for a warship called HMS BRISTOL?	
5.	Move back to ladder opposite Cabin 1/6. Go up to 03 H (the bridge) Answer the following questions - 1. According to the ship's gyro compass (above the wheel) – what is the ship's heading? 2. Looking at the chart, what is the depth of water under HMS BRISTOL? 3. Looking out of the bridge across the port bow, what shapes can you see on top of the yellow and black post? What might these mean?	

While on board the cadets were provided with accommodation and free spaces for meeting and games rooms. Documents like this were issued to help pass the time. If different units were on board, it was surprising how quickly new friendships could blossom. For many cadets this was their first time on a warship, and it did influence many to make a career of the Royal Navy. (Rob Griffin)

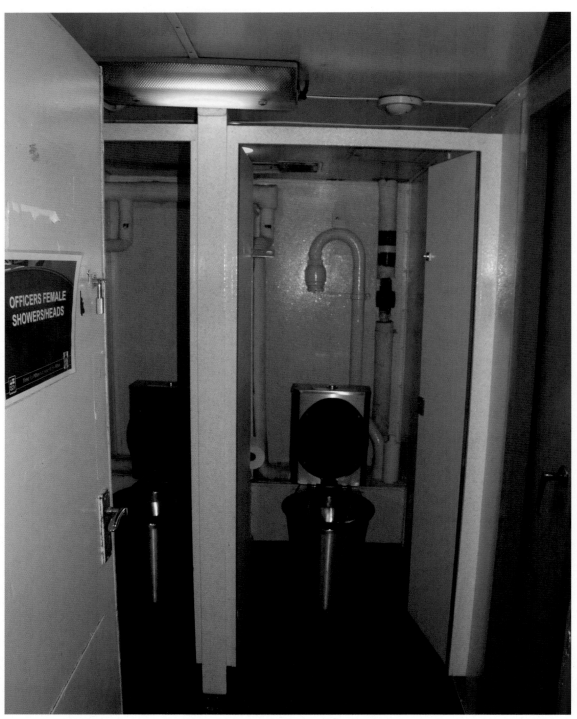

Not exactly five-star luxury but still handy for cadet activities in the local area. The heads (toilets) were unusual in that instead of a simple flush, you had to flush and hold the handle till all flushing was complete; this was because of the way the on-board sewage treatment system worked. (Rob Griffin)

Part of one of the areas designated for cadet entertainment, with the inevitable PC in the corner. (Rob Griffin)

Typical of all the areas in the ship, with plenty of notice boards, Royal Navy photos encouraging recruiting and H&S signage. (Rob Griffin)

The sort of accommodation that greeted the cadets. (Rob Griffin

Another view of a recreation area, showing the large-screen TV. This is one of several areas converted for such use. These could also be used as briefing and lecture rooms, handy with several different units on board. (Rob Griffin)

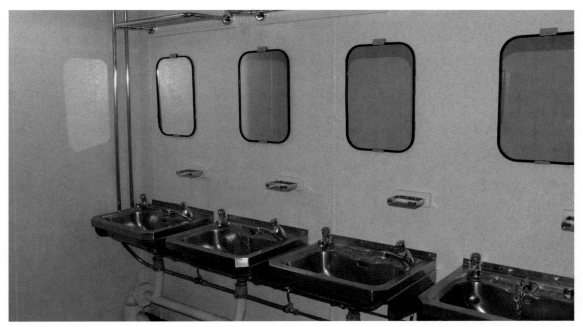

Typical washroom, as used by the cadets. This is one of the features that might have been upgraded if the last refit had taken place. (Rob Griffin)

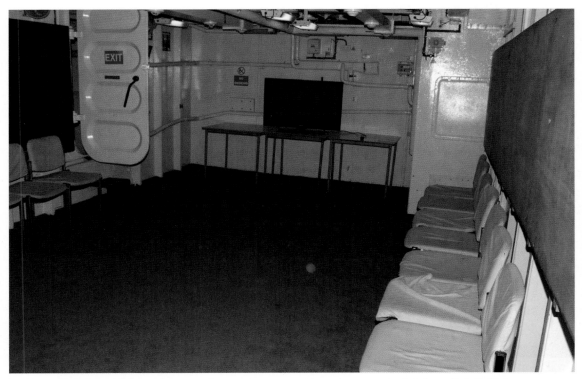

Looking a bit forlorn, this is another area where cadets to can either relax or receive briefings. (Rob Griffin)

This has the appearance of having been a small galley at one time, but no longer in use; the only functioning galley was a small one by the Bristol Lounge and it was for adults only. For all meals staff and cadets had to march from the ship to the top of Whale Island to the main galley, and as the route went past Navy Command Leach Building, they were always guaranteed an admiral or two to salute. (Rob Griffin)

There are several areas that can be used either to relax or to brief cadets on the next activity, as can be seen in this shot. The walls are covered in RN action poses with the unashamed aim of encouraging youngsters to join. (Rob Griffin)

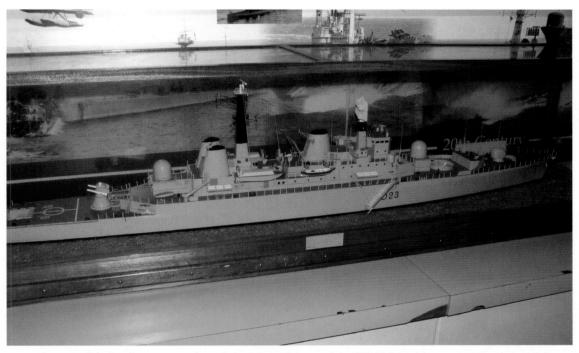

Located in one of the briefing rooms on board, this is one of the models of HMS *Bristol* that are scattered around the ship. (Rob Griffin)

Whilst these areas are not what they used to be, at least they still resound to life and activity. (Rob Griffin)

Although many things were changed to adapt *Bristol* to her new role, some were left in place: this is in the wardroom that is still very much a formal location. The cross-stitch of HMS *Bristol*'s ship's crest was produced by the Gloucester Sea Cadets Admin Officer and was presented to the commanding officer. (Rob Griffin)

It is not just Sea Cadet groups that make use of HMS *Bristol* facilities; this group of Gloucestershire army cadets look as if they are enjoying their stay aboard. (Rob Griffin)

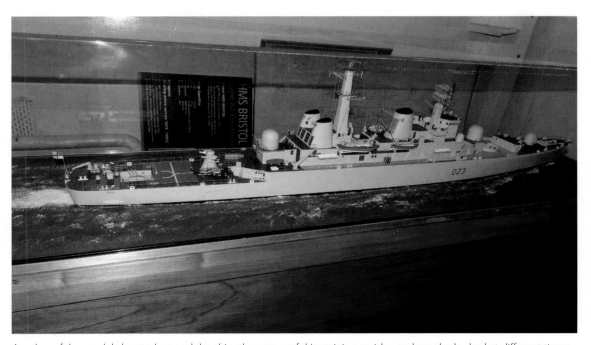

Another of the models located around the ship; they are useful in gaining an idea on how she looked at different times in her career. (Rob Griffin)

Looking more like a building site, this does show just how much work goes into what may seem just a simple refit. (HMS *Bristol*)

An unusual shot of an area not often seen even by the ship's company. Items to be removed as of no further use were her two propellors – the only time Bristol would be at sea again would be in the company of tugs. (HMS *Bristol*)

These Sea Cadets look as if they are having a great time judging by the smiles on their faces. Interestingly, the PO is now in the Royal Navy while the cadets are all now adult instructors. (Rob Griffin)

Officer of the Day nightmare: the Sea Cadets have taken over the bridge, which is a good experience for them as it is normally off limits. (Rob Griffin)

left Portsmouth under tow on 20 October 2010 and left for the return to Portsmouth in April 2011. This refit kept her going and it was proposed that she would receive one more refit before being disposed of. Items that could have been changed were the inclusion of unisex heads as requested by schools in line with modern thinking, and new furniture, neither of which took place when the refit was cancelled.

CHAPTER 7

A SERVICE OF THANKSGIVING ON THE
OCCASION OF THE DECOMMISSIONING OF

HMS BRISTOL

Whale Island, Portsmouth
Wednesday 28 October 2020

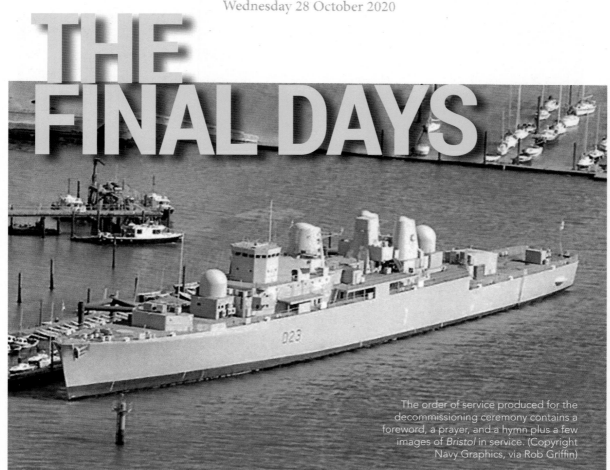

THE FINAL DAYS

The order of service produced for the decommissioning ceremony contains a foreword, a prayer, and a hymn plus a few images of *Bristol* in service. (Copyright Navy Graphics, via Rob Griffin)

So, we come to the end of our voyage with HMS *Bristol*, but as of February 2020, what did the future hold for her? She was due to go into Portsmouth dockyard for a short refit which would have seen things like new furniture and modern unisex toilets, along with other repairs as required. This was designed to give her at least another few years' carrying out her role of harbour accommodation and training ship, until such time as a replacement could be found for her. It is inevitable that eventually she will finish her time under the White Ensign and will have to be replaced; she is 51 years old now and is showing it for she is just a mere shadow of her original proud self – gone are the masts, radar, 4.5-inch gun and Sea Dart launcher. She has served generations of trainees and cadet forces admirably, but all good things must come to an end. The onset of the first COVID lockdown probably hastened her end as well.

Thursday, 13 February 2020 is a date that will be remembered by all those who have an affection for HMS *Bristol*, for despite hopes and positive rumours the axe finally fell. The following is the release from Navy Command:

> Through your Cadet and Youth organisations, you will be aware that during the Annual Budget Cycle the Royal Navy routinely evaluates options and potential adjustment measures to produce a balanced programme which ensures the RN's contribution to Defence is affordable and balances military, programme, and financial risk.
>
> As part of this process the RN has examined the future of HMS BRISTOL in the delivery of internal core training and as a training and accommodation platform for MOD Sponsored Cadet Forces and Youth organisations. I write to you now to inform you that the decision has been made to

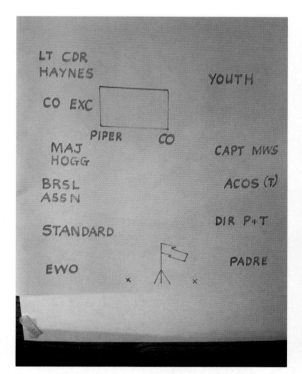

The very simple, almost crude drawing showing the locations of those present at the ceremony. (Peter Featherstone Williams)

The HMS Bristol Association standard bearer Dick Shanton, before the ceremony. (Peter Featherstone Williams)

Some of the representatives from the Royal Navy lined up with the padre at the extreme end of the line. (Peter Featherstone Williams)

Representatives from youth groups who had used *Bristol* throughout her service as harbour training ship, with the Sea Cadets represented nearest the camera. (Peter Featherstone Williams)

One special guest was Major Theo Hogg, the grandson of Lady Hogg who launched *Bristol* in 1969. (Peter Featherstone Williams)

cancel HMS BRISTOL's life extension. As a result, we anticipate that December 2020 will be the final month that HMS BRISTOL will be available for provision of training and accommodation to all users.

I recognise both the significant impact this decision will have on your organisation, and the importance of retaining the RN's close relationships with Youth and Cadet Organisations. As such, I should reassure you of our continued commitment to our Youth and Cadet organisations and of my intent to work together to examine future opportunities to support your outputs.

Two of HMS *Bristol's* crew waiting for the sad moment when her White Ensign is lowered for the last time; even the weather looks sad. (Peter Featherstone Williams)

The final moments of HMS *Bristol* flying the White Ensign, as it is lowered for the last time. (Peter Featherstone Williams)

Peter Featherston Williams, Chairman of HMS *Bristol* Association, receiving the White Ensign. (Peter Featherstone Williams)

HMS *Bristol* Association standard bearer Dick Shanton marches to his position in preparation for the decommissioning service. (Peter Featherstone Williams)

Dick Shanton looking over his old ship which is well into the process of having anything of use removed. (Peter Featherstone Williams)

The cadets' games area is devoid of excited voices and looks desolate with all the packing boxes lying around. (Peter Featherstone Williams)

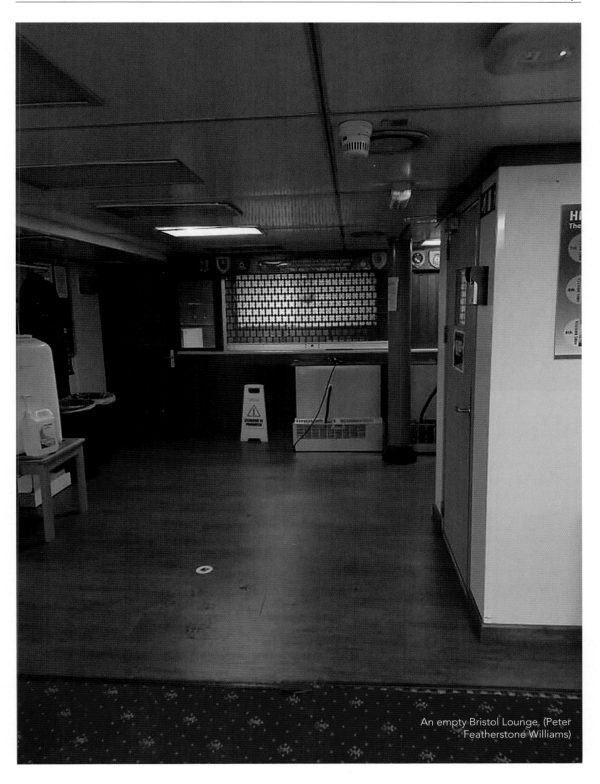

An empty Bristol Lounge. (Peter Featherstone Williams)

HMS *Bristol*, with no Union Jack or White Ensign, quietly awaits her fate. (Damien Burke/ HandmadeByMachine.com)

Her fate was now inevitable, and although just three days after the announcement people were looking to save her, as she is the very last ship from the Falklands task force in the UK, but the problem of preserving an ex-warship is immense and very costly, if we look at the efforts and money expended to try and save the former HMS Hermes which ended in failure. *Bristol* is in a very poor state and would need a lot spent on her if she were to remain a floating museum. Until the end of December 2020 many meetings took place, to decide her fate, and even now in 2022, that is still not cast in stone. What will replace her is another matter, as there are no ships to be taken up, and even with *Bristol* gone, courses for both RN and Cadets will still have to take place; one of the excellent reasons for her continued existence was the use of her accommodation.

So sadly, on 28 October 2020 HMS *Bristol* was finally decommissioned from the Royal Navy, earlier than anticipated and due to the Covid restrictions the numbers attending were limited: the ship's company and HMS Bristol Association were represented; also in attendance was Major Theo Hogg, grandson of Lady Hogg, the ship's sponsor. Once the White Ensign had been hauled down for the very last time, the work to de-store the ship continued and soon she was an empty silent hulk, devoid of power, and awaiting her final fate. Whatever that is she will be missed and will be a sad loss to the hundreds of young people who stayed on her.

During her life HMS *Bristol* steamed 478,671 miles or 40 times round the world; total hours spent underway: 37,601, or four years at sea. Certainly In a Class of Her Own.

POSTSCRIPT

On 23 March 2022 I found myself back aboard HMS *Bristol*, now a hulk, and what a sad place, silent and still, with no sounds of the ventilation fans or voices. To walk through the ship a very bright torch is required as there is no power at all and orange safety lines run through all the compartments and every step has to be taken with care. It felt strange to see areas that had been vibrant and full of life, empty of fittings, but one could almost stand there and hear the voices of those who had enjoyed the ship, either as a full operational warship or the excited cries from Cadets as they enjoyed their time aboard. Altogether a strange experience, and for certain we shall not see the likes of her again.

Familiar to all who visited her during her Sea Cadets/ harbour training days, HQ1 is where all persons were booked in by the civilian security staff. (Rob Griffin)

A rather forlorn-looking Bristol Lounge, with all its furniture removed; this area again was from its training days. (Rob Griffin)

The bar in the Bristol Lounge, always welcome at the end of a day for a quiet drink. The sign above the bar now resides safely in my home. (Rob Griffin)

During his working days on board as CO, I bet Lieutenant-Commander Price never saw his desk this clear! (Rob Griffin)

Rank has its privileges they say: the only bath on board was provided for the CO, almost like the eerie shots of the bath on the *Titanic* in its own way. (Rob Griffin)

APPENDIX

The Captains

Captain R. D. McDonald CBE RN	1972–3
Captain H. P. Janion RN	1973–5
Captain R. R. Squires RN	1975–6
Commander G. E. Liardet RN	1976–7
Captain A. F. R. Weir RN	1977–8
Captain D. W. Brown RN	1978–9
Captain A. Casdagli RN	1979–81
Captain A. Grose RN	1981–2
Captain M. J. F. Rawlinson	1982–3
Captain G. F. Walwyn CVO ADC RN	1983–4
Commander T. W. Loughran RN	1984
Commander H. F. Spencer RN	1984–5
Commander B. C. Murray RN	1985
Commander R. Harding RN	1985
Captain H. M. White CBE RN	1985–7
Captain A. W. J. West DSC RN	1987–8
Captain P. M. Franklyn MVO RN	1988–90
Captain R. Hastilow RN	1990–3
Lieutenant-Commander B. Harper RN	1993
Lieutenant-Commander G. S. Appleyard RN	1993–5
Lieutenant-Commander L. P. Carlton RN	1995–7
Lieutenant-Commander P. R. lewis MBE RN	1997–8
Lieutenant-Commander T. A. Gibson MBE	1998–2000
Lietuenant Commander M. D. Kent RN	2000–2
Lieutenant-Commander R. P. W. Bell RN	2002–5
Liieutenant Commander R. M. Seymour MBE RN	2005–6
Lieutenant-Commander J. W. Haynes RN	2006–8
Lieutenant-Commander A. J. Elston RN	2008–10
Lieuttenant Commander N. A. Storey RN	2010–12
Lieutenant-Commander M. J. Mowles RN	2012
Lieutenant-Commander D. J. Price RN	2012–20